PRESCRIPTION DEATH

Compassionate Killers in the Medical Profession

Prescription Death

Compassionate Killers in the Medical Profession

by Dr. Reed Bell
with Frank York

HUNTINGTON HOUSE PUBLISHERS

Copyright © 1993
All rights reserved. No part of this book may be reproduced without permission from the publisher, except by a reviewer who may quote brief passages in a review; nor may any part of this book be reproduced, stored in a retrieval system or copied by mechanical photocopying, recording or other means, without permission from the publisher.

Huntington House Publishers
P.O. Box 53788
Lafayette, Lousiana 70505

Library of Congress Card Catalog Number 93-78387
ISBN 1-56384-045-6

Dedication

To my wife Nell—
who bespeaks wisdom borne of life's experience; who upholds her faith in righteous living and service to her marriage, her family and her community; whose incredible good humor, wit and common sense invite joy; who speaks the truth in love; whose strength and courage inspires virtue; and whose love is boundless.

Thank you, my one true love,

Reed

Contents

ONE	The Death Ethic in Medicine	9
TWO	The Destruction of Unworthy Life	25
THREE	The Crisis in American Medical Ethics	35
FOUR	Feminism: Killing Families	49
FIVE	Killing the Unborn	73
SIX	Killing Handicapped Newborns	89
SEVEN	Killing as Medical Treatment	107
EIGHT	AIDS: Killing by Medical Neglect	129
NINE	Bioethics and the New Pagans	149
TEN	Doctors: Licensed to Kill	165
APPENDIX A	When Does Life Begin?	179
APPENDIX B	A Pro-life Perspective on Abortion	189
APPENDIX C	Suicide: Any Limits to Self-Autonomy?	205
	Organizations	217
	Recommended Reading	218
	Notes	220

Chapter 1

The Death Ethic in Medicine

Will your physician kill you some day? The question is not one to be taken lightly or brushed off as an absurd possibility. If current trends in medical ethics continue, your doctor may eventually be authorized by the government to perform *medicide* upon you—planned death—either at your request or perhaps against your will, if the doctor deems such treatment to be needed.

In the last twenty years, a death ethic has evolved in American medicine that has ominous parallels to the ethics of the Nazi doctors under Adolf Hitler's regime. This new ethic puts relative value on life, the quality of life rather than on the absolute value of life. It advocates compassionate killing as a way of solving personal, social, economic, and medical problems.

The concept of assisted dying is couched in the most compassionate terms, but the result is always a dead person. Those who advocate aid-in-dying use such terms as death with dignity, the right to die, choice in dying, termination of pregnancy, or mercy killing, but the helpless individual who is the target of this compassion ends up dead.

Regrettably, our medical establishment is slowly, but surely, accepting the idea that physician assistance in dying—killing the patient—is a legitimate medical procedure.

Presently, we face a concerted effort to legalize assisting terminally ill and severely disabled patients to die, which is termed physician assisted suicide (euthanasia). The killing of unwanted ,unborn children—abortion—of course has been legal since 1973. There was an effort in 1982 to sanction the killing of handicapped newborn children (infanticide). As a pediatrician involved in bioethics issues with the American Academy of Pediatrics (AAP) during that time, I became involved in what proved to be a major deterrent to infanticide, the Baby Doe case.

In 1982, a Downs syndrome baby was born in Bloomington, Indiana. This is not an unusual occurrence, but in this case, Baby Doe made national headlines and caused an uproar in the medical community. Why? Baby Doe was not only a Downs syndrome child, but had a congenital malformation of his esophagus (food pipe), which a routine surgical procedure could have readily repaired. Unfortunately, Baby Doe's parents and doctor chose to allow the infant to starve because of the grim prospect of a mentally retarded child. This case was appealed to the Indiana Supreme Court, where the court upheld the right of the parents to allow their infant to be starved to death.

Right-to-life groups, disability groups, the Association for Retarded Citizens, and the U.S. Department of Health and Human Services attempted to intervene to protect the life of Baby Doe, but none was successful.

This case caused a worldwide furor and led to the formation of myriad medical ethics groups. In the forefront was the bioethics committee of the American Academy of Pediatrics, which undertook the task of establishing legal and procedural safeguards for the protection of handicapped newborns.

I was privileged to have been one of six doctors assigned to that committee, and we spent the next two years working out detailed guidelines to protect other

Baby Does from being allowed to die by neglect, or even assisted in dying.

In December of 1983, the American Academy of Pediatrics and eight disability groups issued a joint statement declaring that:
- Discrimination against anyone with a disability, regardless of its severity, is morally and legally indefensible;
- Disabled individuals have the same rights as any other citizen, rights recognized at birth;
- A person's disability (mental or physical) must not be the basis for withholding treatment;
- Anticipated limited potential or lack of community resources are irrelevant and must not determine decisions concerning medical care;
- The individual's medical condition should be the sole focus of the decision.

As a pediatrician for more than twenty-five years, the Baby Doe case brought me face to face with what I had not fully comprehended: That something terribly wrong was developing in the medical profession. Our ethics were changing. We were slowly leaving our calling as healers, we were being encouraged to allow patients to die by neglect or non-treatment, and we were considering provisions for assistance in dying. The shades of Karl Binding's 1920 essay darkened my thoughts. Entitled *Releasing Persons from Lives Devoid of Value,* it set the stage for the pogroms of Nazi Germany.[1] (We will discuss how this essay impacted the German medical profession in the next chapter.)

The Quality of Life Ethic

Although I am no longer on the bioethics committee, I am a member of an educational section that examines bioethical issues for the AAP, addressing numerous life treatment and death issues. What I have discovered since becoming a participant in bioethics activities is that a number of medical ethicists and philosophers have indoctrinated our profession with the idea that life is not sacrosanct; it is relative, dependent on its quality. One of those ethicists is Peter Singer, who wrote in the July 1983 issue of *Pediatrics* that if we compare a dog or a pig to a severely defective infant, we often find the non-human to have superior capacities. To Singer, being a member of the human race is not morally superior to being a dog or a pig. He believes that the idea of sanctity of human life is simply religious mumbo-jumbo, which must be discarded in favor of the so-called quality of life ethic.

This new quality of life ethic is revealed in a statement made by Nobel Laureate James Watson:

> Because of the present limits of such detection methods, most birth defects are not discovered until birth. If a child were not declared alive until three days after birth, then all parents could be allowed the choice . . . the doctor could allow the child to die if the parents so choose and save a lot of misery and suffering.[2]

Fortunately, our bioethics committee was successful in aiding the establishment of safeguards for newborns through child abuse legislation. This prompted the formation of bioethics committees in hospitals across the U.S. The executive director of the AAP, Dr. Jim Strain; Surgeon General C. Everett Koop; and President Reagan became vitally instrumental in helping to provide protection for handicapped infants and children who would otherwise have been neglected in intensive care units of hospitals or other child care facilities.

While we were successful in slowing down the trend toward the infanticide of handicapped newborns, we have not been successful in dealing with a number of other serious life and death issues facing the medical profession.

Presently, we face an effort by pro-death activists like Derek Humphry, founder of the Hemlock Society, a nonprofit group organized to promote all manners of suicide, and Dr. Jack Kevorkian (dubbed Dr. Death in the media), the maverick physician illegally assisting patients in suicide, to legalize suicide-on-demand as a patient's right, physician-assisted suicide, and voluntary and non-voluntary euthanasia for those whose quality of life is deemed unworthy or burdensome. And, of course, the defining issue of abortion-on-demand (feticide) persists as a woman's right to choice—killing of the unborn infant.

As doctors and as a society, we must come to grips with these serious life and death treatment and nontreatment issues. As our culture is further inculcated with the pro-death ethic, doctors are going to be the ones expected to carry out the sentence of death upon those whose lives are not considered worthy to be lived. We must resist the ideology of the Derek Humphrys, the Kevorkians, the Singers, and Watsons who see no unique value to individual human life, superseding the utility of the individual's function.

The Way We Were

Not so many years ago, our profession was held to high ethical standards. I can recall attending Duke Medical School in the late forties and early fifties and being taught that our duty as doctors was to heal, alleviate pain, and serve our community. We were taught that it was our obligation to treat patients, even those who couldn't pay for our services. We were, in a sense, ministers.

As a general intern at Cincinnati General Hospital, I was involved in providing indigent health care services as part of my training. In fact, as I entered private practice in 1957, part of the by-laws of the local county medical society stated that as professionals we were required to provide uncompensated care to the indigent and medically needy. As a doctor, I was expected to serve as the advocate for all of my patients. It was my obligation to make sure they received adequate health care.

As doctors educated and trained in this ethical context, it never occurred to us that we wouldn't treat the poor. It also never occurred to us that abortion, infanticide, suicide, and euthanasia were ever options for doctors committed to the Hippocratic Oath. Regrettably, this oath has come to be mostly ignored by the medical profession as we have drifted toward a materialistic, utilitarian ethic.

I believe it is essential for the medical profession to take a serious look at where this new ethic is leading us. We are going the way of dehumanization, which always precedes human atrocities. (More on this in the next chapter.)

The reestablishment of the Hippocratic Oath in the medical profession is an important way to stop the drift toward a death ethic that will institutionalize killing as a way of solving personal, social, economic, and medical problems.

The Hippocratic Oath

The Rev. Nigel Cameron, in his book, *The New Medicine*, discusses the importance of the Hippocratic Oath and the dangers to the medical profession as a result of its elimination as an ethical statement for doctors.

The oath itself is attributed to Hippocrates, a fifth century B.C. Greek physician who developed the statement as a radical departure from the kind of medicine practiced in Greece at the time. In fifth century B.C. Greece, abortion, infanticide, physician-assisted suicide, and euthanasia were commonplace. Hippocrates apparently thought that the role of the physician should be a high calling—one that valued human life as sacred and the physician as healer.

As anthropologist Margaret Mead pointed out, the Hippocratic Oath marked a change in which

> for the first time in our tradition there was a complete separation between killing and curing. Throughout the primitive world the doctor and sorcerer tended to be the same person. He with the power to kill had power to cure . . . He who had power to cure would necessarily also be able to kill.
>
> With the Greeks, the distinction was made clear. One's profession . . . was to be dedicated completely to life

under all circumstances, regardless of rank, age, or intellect—the life of a slave, the life of the Emperor, the life of a foreign man, the life of a defective child . . . but society always is attempting to make the physician into a killer—to kill the defective child at birth, to leave the sleeping pills beside the bed of the cancer patient . . .[3]

The Hippocratic Oath marked a dramatic departure in the practice of medicine, and its impact has been felt for more than two thousand years in Western civilization. As Nigel Cameron observes, "Hippocratism is healing and not harming."[4]

Our profession has lost a great deal by first modifying and then abandoning the tenets of the Hippocratic Oath. For the reader who is unfamiliar with the oath, let me quote it here:

> *I swear by Apollo Physician, by Asclepius, by Hygeia, by Panaceia, and by all the gods and goddesses, making them witnesses, that I will carry out, according to my ability and judgment, this oath and this indenture:*
>
> *To regard my teacher in this art as equal to my parents; to make him partner in my livelihood, and when he is in need of money to share mine with him; to consider his offspring equal to my brothers; to teach them this art, if they require to learn it, without fee or indenture; and to impart precept, oral instruction, and all the other learning, to my sons, to the sons of my teacher, and to pupils who have signed the indenture and sworn obedience to the physician's Law, but to none other.*
>
> *I will use treatment to help the sick according to my ability and judgment, but I will never use it to injure or wrong them.*
>
> *I will not give poison to anyone though asked to do so, nor will I suggest such a plan. Similarly I will not give a pessary to a woman to cause abortion. But in purity and in holiness I will guard my life and my art.*
>
> *I will not use the knife either on sufferers from stone, but will give place to such as are craftsmen therein.*

Into whatsoever house I enter, I will do so to help the sick, keeping myself free from all intentional wrong-doing and harm, especially from fornication with woman or man, bond or free.

Whatsoever in the course of practice I see or hear (or even outside my practice in social intercourse) that ought never to be published abroad, I will not divulge, but consider such things to be holy secrets.

Now if I keep this oath and break it not, may I enjoy honor, in my life and art, among all men for all time; but if I transgress and forswear myself, may the opposite befall me.

The oath was a moral statement, a value-based judgment, secular in origin, that bound the physician to avoid providing abortions or aid-in-dying. It also pledged the healer to avoid harming his patient either through sexual misconduct or betraying a confidence because of his advocacy relationship with his patient and the intimate trust the patient ultimately places in him.

As I was going through medical school (1948-1951), the oath was never specifically mentioned in any class I attended, but it was generally understood to be the basis upon which we were to practice medicine. But times have changed, and a "New Medicine" is being practiced—one that closely resembles the pagan medicine that existed prior to the Hippocratic Oath. Pagan medicine allowed the doctor to be both healer and killer—a shaman or witch doctor—who held both life and death in his hands.

It is my belief that if we do not return to a sanctity of life ethic in medicine, we will become no better than the Nazi doctors who performed grisly experiments on concentration camp inmates. Unfortunately, there is ample evidence that grisly experiments have already been performed on live, aborted children and spina bifida babies have been victimized by death-ethic doctors.

Attorney John Whitehead in *The Stealing of America*, for example, describes an experiment conducted by Dr. Peter A. J. Adam, an associate professor of pediatrics at Case Western Reserve University in 1973. Adam reported his experiment to the American Pediatric Society for Research on a study he and his associates had conducted on twelve babies (up to twenty gestational weeks old) who had been born alive by hysterotomy abortion. These research doctors took the babies, cut off their heads, and placed tubes inside the internal carotid arteries to keep the heads alive.

Adam observed, "Once society's declared the fetus dead, and abrogated its rights, I don't see any ethical problem. . . . Whose rights are we going to protect, once we've decided the fetus won't live?"[5]

Ten years later, *Pediatrics* magazine (4 October 1983) reported on a team of specialists at the University of Oklahoma who evaluated sixty-nine newborn babies who had spina bifida. They admitted that these defects could have been corrected, but decided to use a mathematical equation to decide whether to initiate treatment. Values such as the child's quality of life, his or her estimated intelligence, and the availability of support from home and from society were inserted into the equation, and a scale was derived to determine treatment or non-treatment.

On the basis of this evaluation, they treated thirty-six of the sixty-nine infants, and they all did well. The remaining twenty-four babies were given no surgery, no shunt, no antibiotics, and allowed to die.[6]

As John Whitehead has observed in *The Second American Revolution*,

> With abortion, infanticide, and euthanasia, the doctor ceases to be the protector of life and becomes a murderer, even if the Supreme Court says it is legal. A radical change is taking place in the medical profession. Instead of regarding life as sacrosanct—as wholly governed by God and beyond the doctor's province to destroy—doctors have begun to play God. The doctor becomes a murderer just as the judge who legitimizes abortion is a murderer.[7]

Family Breakdown

For nineteen years I served as director of the Sacred Heart Children's Hospital in Pensacola, Florida. During my tenure there, I was in charge of developing a pediatric residency training program and helped establish a critical care facility for newborns and children. Also, during this time, I became an active advocate for children as a representative of the pediatric community.

As one who has been actively involved in the hospital care of newborns and children, I have noted another alarming trend. The breakdown of the family has resulted in an ever-increasing incidence of neglect in meeting the personal, social, and health needs of children. It was heart-breaking and gut-wrenching to release children from our hospital, knowing they were going back to homes where they would be neglected and receive minimal or no nurturing or love. It became obvious to me that the loss of stable family life was going to result in ever higher levels of unmet needs in caring for children.

I recall sitting in meeting after meeting of government officials, community leaders, social workers, and health care professionals as they discussed the need for new programs to deal with a growing health care crisis, especially among children. When all was said and done, however, it was obvious that only a restoration of the two-parent family would ultimately solve the crisis we face. Yet well-meaning officials, social workers, and physicians seemed oblivious to this fact.

At that point in my career, I decided that I would become actively pro-family and do whatever I could to see that pro-family policies were implemented in the children's programs in Florida. Government programs can't substitute for a healthy home life and represent only marginally helpful intervention, not prevention, in the progressive decline of the well-being of infants, children, and adolescents.

Technology and Economics

During the past thirty years, the medical profession has seen incredible advances in technology in the diagnosis and treatment of our patients. Along with this technological advance has come increasing pressures to contain medical costs. Combined, these two factors have contributed immeasurably to the idea of rationing health care. Some medical ethicists believe we should set limits on who should be treated and for how long. Some have even suggested that we stop providing medical care to those over seventy-five years of age.

With our growing elderly population, there are more and more pressures being placed upon doctors to discontinue medical and surgical care. With terminally ill patients, for example, the patient's self-autonomous right to refuse treatment, including sustenance, is always honored. The patient's choice, if they are competent (or if they are not competent, the family's substituted judgment), is honored as to withholding and/or withdrawing care, including food and water. Physician paternalism is discounted, and these concepts of patient self-determination and substituted judgments reign in decision-making. These concepts have expanded and are applied to states of irreversible coma, the persistent vegetative state (PVS) constituting acceptance of passive voluntary and nonvoluntary euthanasia.

It is estimated that there are ten thousand people in a persistent vegetative state in the U.S. Many ethicists, doctors, and health care officials are arguing that these people should all be allowed to die. There are others who would argue that the senile, severely disabled, demented, and mentally ill should also be allowed to die—or even be assisted in dying to conserve and more justly allocate scarce resources. The argument is always that it is in the best interest of these individuals to be provided death. The danger is that there will be an ever-expanding circle of burdensome, or unwanted, individuals (i.e., those whose lives are not worthy to be lived). The slippery slope argument is a valid one, as we will see in the next chapter on Nazi medicine.

The trend in condoning suicide and euthanasia in the U.S. is towards providing procedural safeguards and guidelines to prevent abuses of the service provider's authority. These guidelines euphemistically legitimize a practice that can only be defined as condoned suicide, physician-assisted suicide, and voluntary or non-voluntary euthanasia. The only remaining venue for death to be considered as a solution is involuntary euthanasia—homicide. How long before this becomes a legitimate option?

The Jack Kevorkians and Derek Humphrys are not going to be content until they see the establishment of obitiary clinics all over the country to provide individuals with the "right to die," a planned death (medicide). Introduction of this medical service into our society would motivate certain elements in our profession to prosper by systematically relieving suffering via "compassionate killing"—the so-called good death of euthanasia.

The new minimalist ethic is in place—individual choice or radical autonomy—along with a materialistic, hedonistic, utilitarian ethos guiding our culture, aided and abetted by some hard economic times. There remains only the barrier of the outmoded sanctity of life to prevent implementation of death solutions should abortion be joined by obitiary services as a convenience.

Children's Rights Movement

I first faced these ethical dilemmas in the early 1980s when I was called upon to treat children with brain injury or newborns with severe congenital birth defects. With new critical care technology, such as ventilators that breathe for children and neonatal intensive care, the child's chances of living with a good outcome were greatly improved. But what of the costs involved? Should I have allowed these infants to die? Was I simply prolonging dying? Was I preserving lives of an unacceptable quality? In fact, should I have actually assisted some in dying?

In the seventies and eighties, there appeared an aggressive move by child advocates to restructure the relationship between parents, the child, and the doctor. In our medical tradition, parental notification and informed consent has been legally required before granting medical/surgical services to a minor, except in an emergency. To do otherwise is considered battery. This was abrogated only if the parent's interests were clearly counter to the best interests of the child and required a court ruling.

Children's rights advocates, however, began viewing children as having choice rights to assent and consent to health care, superseding the protective rights of children and parental prerogative. They claim that children should have entitlement rights to confidential health care from birth, not from the age of majority. They believe children should be liberated from their parents when it comes to health care decisions.

This issue centered largely on the controversy over parental notification and/or parental consent laws dealing with adolescent contraception and abortion. The public health sector, professional groups, and Planned Parenthood advocates empowered by the children's rights movement were largely successful in separating the parent from the adolescent youth in provision of abortion and contraception services.

Today, the medical profession tends to view adolescent health care relationships as a private one between the physician and the teen-ager. As a result of this changed relationship, we can expect to see a continued growth in school-based health clinics, which will dispense contraceptives, refer for abortions, provide sexual counseling (including homosexuality as an acceptable alternative lifestyle), and other services, with or without parental knowledge or consent.

Behavior-based Health Problems

When I was a shore patrolman in the U.S. Navy in Chicago at the end of World War II, I spent a good deal of my time rounding up intoxicated marines and getting them back to their base or directing them to sexually transmitted disease (STD) clinics for treatment of gonorrhea, syphilis, or other exotic diseases picked up by sexual activity. As I sat in the waiting room hearing these men agonize because gonorrhea had infected their urethras, I became acutely aware of the kind of pain and despair that can result from a behavior-related disease.

Today, our nation, its youth in particular, faces an epidemic of such behavior-related diseases unprecedented in modern times. We face an HIV/AIDS epidemic that results overwhelmingly from I.V. drug use and anal sexual behavior. Our teen-agers face pregnancies resulting from premature and promiscuous sexuality, and the bottom line of the sexual revolution is millions of cases of venereal disease each year. The situation does not seem to be getting any better. Those who advocate a return to abstinence before marriage and fidelity in marriage are ridiculed by health education professionals and groups like Planned Parenthood or SIECUS (Sex Information and Education Council of the U.S.). We are facing a major medical crisis among our teen-agers with STDs and unwanted pregnancies, but the solution, as always, seems to be more government programs, more health education funding, more school-based health clinics, and condom distribution. The safe sex message holds sway. "We know you're going to have sex, here's a condom."

The most productive message we can give our teens is to inform them of the dangers of premarital sex and tell them very clearly that they should abstain from sexual intercourse until they marry. This is an old-fashioned message yet the best form of preventative medicine available. We do not have a confused message about cigarette smoking, drunk driving, or drug use. We should convey the same message about premarital sexual activity.

Unfortunately, the pro-abortion movement has a financial stake in keeping abortion legal. Millions of dollars of income would be at risk if a pure abstinence message were widely accepted. Planned Parenthood and other family planning groups would go out of business if they couldn't continue to provide contraceptives, engage in abortion referrals, and promote condom-mania.

Radical Autonomy

The pro-death movement within the medical profession is an outgrowth of a philosophical viewpoint that has gained many adherents within medicine, government, media, academia, and other power centers in our culture.

This viewpoint has many different names, often referred to as liberation, libertarianism, or radical autonomy. Simply stated, radical autonomy holds that each individual is solely responsible for his own behavior; he is to be allowed as much freedom as possible to express himself, and this freedom should be almost unlimited, unless it is harmful to others or if he is coerced. The advocate of radical autonomy denies that the individual has any responsibility to others or the community. He believes that the individual's freedom must be protected, even if that behavior is harmful to the individual.

The autonomous man, therefore, should have the unrestricted right to kill himself if he wishes. He should have the right to engage in sexual behavior of any form as long as chosen freely or autonomously. His freedom is nearly absolute, albeit chosen and uncoerced. To the radical autonomist, there are no moral absolutes. Concepts of right and wrong are irrelevant; if an action is something the person desires, it is good as long as it does no harm to others.

With this philosophy in a dominant position within the medical profession, it is not surprising that abortion on demand exists as a woman's autonomous right and that the aggressive movement within the profession is gaining speed in its efforts to legalize death on demand as a fundamental right.

I would not be surprised to someday see an abortion

clinic also offering planned death as one of its clinical services. The individual could go into the obitiary clinic and be killed by lethal injection whenever chosen. It would be a constitutional right for an autonomous individual. This service, of course, could be offered to teenagers without parental consent or knowledge as the right of a legally emancipated minor to access health care—and be funded by tax dollars!

This scenario is not as far-fetched as it might seem. A law was passed in 1992 in Connecticut that allows teenagers to receive an HIV/AIDS test without parental consent or knowledge. And teens are already allowed by most states to be treated for sexually transmitted diseases, procure contraception services, and obtain abortions. If the trend continues, it may be only a matter of time before death on demand is considered legitimate medical treatment.

The death ethic that has permeated our medical profession parallels ominously to what occurred in pre-Nazi Germany during the 1920s and 1930s. In the next chapter, we'll look at what happened to Germany's doctors. Think of it as looking back to the future.

Chapter 2

The Destruction of Unworthy Life

Ideas have consequences. The philosophical ideas that provided the justification for the mass murder of millions of Jews, Poles, Russians, and other enemies of the Nazi state seeped into the national consciousness of Germany in a number of ways.

One of those avenues was through the university professors who taught the philosophies of Georg Hegel and others. The disciples of these philosophers taught that it was impossible to know truth and that moral absolutes could not exist. Everything that exists, according to Hegel, is in a process of change. No one can know God or truly discern whether something is right or wrong. It depends upon the circumstance.

This philosophy effectively undercut the Christian belief in a Creator God and moral absolutes, ultimately leading the German people into one of the most devastating wars in the history of the world.

Related to this secular philosophy was the worship of the state as the absolute source of authority in German society. Adolf Hitler once exclaimed that "The needs of the state are the sole determining factors. What may be necessary today need not be so tomorrow." The dictatorship of the state then determined what Hegel called "rational utility." If a policy worked and strengthened the state, it was good; if it did not work, it was wrong. This same Hegelian philosophy also influenced Karl Marx and led him to develop a philosophy that has resulted in the ongoing deaths of millions during the twentieth century.

Another philosophical strain that impacted the German people—and especially the doctors—came from a revolutionary essay that was published in 1920 by Dr. Alfred Hoche and jurist Karl Binding. The essay, *Releasing Persons from Lives Devoid of Value*, recommended a new medical ethic in dealing with mental patients and others whose lives were considered worthless. Hoche and Binding recommended the killing of useless individuals as a way of saving money and of doing the individual a favor by releasing him from the perceived miseries of a life devoid of value. Hoche and Binding stressed the therapeutic nature of killing by calling it purely a healing treatment and a healing work.

In Binding's section, he discussed the doctor's responsibility in death assistance and the killing of the consenting participant, as well as killing those unable to consent. He recommended that a three-person panel be established to accept applications from those wishing to die.

Hoche introduces the concept of "mental death" to describe the retarded, or those suffering other forms of brain damage. He described these people as human ballast and recommended that killing them would be an allowable, useful act. He maintained that these people were already dead. The doctor's duty was to simply complete the death process by killing the body.

Hoche made a prediction that proved correct—especially in Nazi Germany: "A new age will come which, from the standpoint of a higher morality, will no longer heed the demands of an inflated concept of humanity and an overestimation of the value of life as such."[1]

Medical ethicist Nigel Cameron notes that the euthanasia program, which resulted from the adoption of Binding and Hoche's philosophy, eventually brought about the Holocaust. The euthanasia program, notes Cameron, marked the point at which German medicine withdrew from many centuries of western Hippocratic consensus.[2]

The doctor as healer quickly became the doctor as killer. The justification for killing the handicapped and mentally ill, of course, was that Germany was experiencing hard times, and it was wrong to waste resources on people whose lives were not worth living. The idea crept into the German mindset that killing was a legitimate way to solve internal social, political, and economic problems—and physicians led the way in promoting this idea.

The idea swept through German society with frightening rapidity. In 1931 a group of psychiatrists met in Bavaria to discuss the sterilization and killing of those with chronic mental illnesses. By 1936 the practice of killing the socially unfit was so common that it was mentioned only incidentally in a German medical journal.

The psychiatrists apparently took the leadership in recommending the killing of the mentally ill as a way of relieving the state's economic burdens. They then moved on to kill crippled children, elderly senile, and those with epilepsy or multiple sclerosis. Eventually, they were also killing World War I soldiers who had lost their legs or their mental capacity—after all, in neither case could they effectively defend the German state.

The German people were convinced through propaganda films and the educational system that killing was an effective means of solving social problems. One blatantly pro-euthanasia film was *I Accuse*, which depicts the life history of a woman who is suffering from multiple sclerosis. Her husband, a doctor, finally kills her to the accompaniment of soft piano music played by a friend in an adjoining room.

Mathematics textbooks were used to indoctrinate German children into accepting killing to solve social or economic problems. One math text, *Mathematics in the Service of National Political Education*, gives the students problems dealing with the costs of caring for the chronically ill versus providing those funds for new housing units or marriage-allowance loans. The problem clearly leads the child to conclude that it makes much more economic sense to kill the handicapped in order to give funds to newlyweds.

In July of 1933, not long after Hitler was elected chancellor of Germany, a law for the prevention of progeny with hereditary defects was declared. This law allowed for the compulsory sterilization of those with congenital mental defects, schizophrenia, manic-depressive psychosis, epilepsy, and severe alcoholism.

Dr. Leo Alexander, a Boston psychiatrist, detailed the horrors of the pre-Nazi and Nazi euthanasia program in his 1949 essay, "Medical Science Under Dictatorship," published in the 14 July 1949 *New England Journal of Medicine*. Between 1946 and 1949, Alexander served as a consultant to the secretary of war, on duty in the office of the chief counsel for war crimes, Nuremberg. It was Alexander's job to investigate the direction that medicine and science took in helping to bring about the Jewish Holocaust.[3]

His article is a chilling indictment of the Derek Humphrys and Jack Kevorkians of the world who recommend killing to solve personal and social problems. It deserves a detailed discussion because his analysis of what happened to the medical profession in pre-Nazi Germany is relevant to the ethical issues we're facing in the late twentieth century.

Many people would deny there is any such thing as a slippery slope in medicine, but the Nazi experience is very clear on this point. The German doctors created a brilliant scientific community, but they were the leaders of the killing movement long before Hitler came to power. Before appealing to the government in economic or political considerations, they justified killing as a humane way of relieving human suffering. The argument umbrella widened to include Hitler's concerns only later.

Kevorkian uses the same preliminary argument today to justify helping the chronically ill kill themselves.

Dr. Alexander notes that the first direct order for euthanasia was issued in September 1939 by Hitler. An organization headed by Dr. Karl Brandt was set up to carry out the killing program. Under Brandt's authority, all state institutions were required to report on patients who had been ill five years or more and who were unable to work. The decision to kill was based on this questionnaire detailing a wide range of data from name, race, and marital status to next of kin, whether the patient had visitors, and who the visitors were. The authority to kill was granted by a panel of psychiatry professors at key universities. They never saw the patients. One expert evaluated 2,109 questionnaires between 14 November and 1 December 1940.

These questionnaires were collected by the Realms Work Committee of Institutions for Cure and Care. A Realms Committee for Scientific Approach to Severe Illness Due to Heredity and Constitution was assigned the task of killing children. In addition, the Charitable Transport Company for the Sick transported the victims to the killing centers. The Charitable Foundation for Institutional Care was given the task of collecting the cost of the killings from the relatives.

This bizarre killing program quickly became a major growth industry in Germany. Eventually, more than 275,000 people were put to death in these killing centers. As Alexander notes,

> Ghastly as this seems, it should be realized that this program was merely the entering wedge for exterminations of far greater scope in the political program for genocide of conquered nations and the racially unwanted.[4]

These killing centers grew as the Nazis expanded their vision of killing off entire nations. The plan in Europe was to kill all Jews and Poles and to wipe out 30 million Russians. The Nazis had a special though less deadly plan for England as well. They were going to enslave all English men in labor camps and then take the English women to improve their own Aryan stock.

The extermination program carried on by Dr. Brandt and his fellow physicians resulted in the development of effective poisons to quickly kill large numbers of Jews and other undesirables. One killing enthusiast named Brack developed the idea of making gas chambers look like shower stalls. The Jews would arrive at the killing centers, thinking they were going to labor camps. They were stripped down, given paper shirts, and herded into the gas chambers. Standing under the shower heads, holding their little bars of soap, they soon realized no drains were in the floors and no water was coming from the shower heads. After they were gassed, their bodies were thrown on a conveyor belt and moved into a crematoria. Their ashes were then returned to their relatives.

As the numbers of killings increased, German researchers realized they had an almost unlimited supply of human guinea pigs to use for various scientific experiments. After all, it would not fit in their reasoning not to use this opportunity to develop new medical procedures, which might benefit the German people as a whole.

In his investigation of the Jewish Holocaust, Dr. Alexander interviewed Dr. Hallervorden, who had collected five hundred brains from a killing center for the insane. From 1942 on, it was common knowledge among physicians that medical experiments were freely conducted on concentration camp inmates. This program included what was called terminal human experiments, where the inmate eventually died of his injuries. According to Alexander, a large part of this research was devoted to techniques designed to either kill or prevent life. Research into developing mass sterilization techniques were developed. At Auschwitz, Dr. Karl Clauberg developed a method whereby he could sterilize one thousand women a day.

At Dachau, Dr. Sigmund Rascher conducted research

to develop an effective blood coagulant for German soldiers wounded in battle. He would clock the number of drops of blood coming from a freshly cut amputation of a living prisoner. Another part of his research consisted of shooting Russian prisoners of war in the spleen to see how quickly they would bleed to death.

In the interests of science, Dr. August Hirt, professor of anatomy at the University of Strassburg, expressed concern to Nazi officials that if the entire Jewish race were eliminated, there would be no skulls or skeletons available for future research. He proposed to keep a collection of Jewish skeletons at the university for posterity. He eventually collected 150 bodies, including Jewish Russian soldiers and women from Auschwitz.

Dehumanizing the Victims

How could medical doctors, researchers, and psychiatrists participate in such horrible atrocities? They had been convinced, through incessant propaganda, that all non-Germans were less than human. They were taught that Jews were threats to the economic and social well-being of the Nazi state and that it was the duty of the state to eliminate them. The physicians bought into this philosophy before the German people did. They considered it their duty to the state to help eliminate any perceived threat to the Fatherland. The Nazi slogan, "Jews, lice, typhus," degraded the Jew to the status of a bug or a bacteria that needed to be exterminated for the good of the state.

In order to hide the reality of killing other human beings, the Nazis developed an elaborate new vocabulary to describe their activities. Robert Jay Lifton, in *The Nazi Doctors*, describes the efforts of Nazis to dehumanize the victims by using euphemisms. They would use words like *resettlement, evacuation*, and *possible solution* as euphemisms for killing Jews. The Nazi doctors did not literally believe these euphemisms, said Lifton, but it gave the doctors a discourse in which killing was no longer killing, and need not be experienced, or even perceived, as killing. These euphemisms allowed the doctors to enter into a "realm of derealization, disavowal, and nonfeeling."[5]

The dehumanization of a group of individuals must always precede a decision to kill them. Our own history in the treatment of blacks is a good example of this process. It was necessary for slave owners to consider blacks as less than human in order to justify their enslavement. This same dehumanization process has taken place in considering the rights of unborn children. The feminists and those in the abortion industry had to define the unborn child as a nonperson in order to justify killing the baby.

This dehumanization process flies in the face of the morality of Western civilization, based as it was on the Judeo-Christian belief system. This belief system pointed out that men and women were created in the image of God. We are a special creation of God and have an inalienable right to life. This view of mankind as a creation and reflection of God led to a compassion for the poor, for the helpless, the sick, and the lame. It led to the establishment of hospitals, charitable homes for the destitute, and contributed significantly to our whole concept of inalienable rights under our Constitution and the laws of God.

The Nazi experience, says Leo Alexander, should serve as a warning to the entire medical profession as to how slowly and imperceptibly changes can occur in the way doctors view their patients. This shift among German doctors, says Alexander, began as a subtle shift in the emphasis of the physicians. It started with a viewpoint that there is such a thing as life not worthy to be lived. It began with accepting the elimination of the severely and chronically sick. "Gradually it led to killing the socially unproductive, the ideologically unwanted, the racially unwanted, and finally all non-Germans."[6]

Alexander notes that American physicians must be always on the alert to avoid the Hegelian view of rational utility in dealing with their patients. He observes,

The original concept of medicine and nursing was not based on any rational or feasible likelihood that they could actually cure and restore but rather on an essentially maternal or religious idea.[7]

He warns that doctors are in danger of becoming mere technicians of rehabilitation instead of caring professionals.

Alexander further urges doctors to realize where the medical profession stands on fundamental premises. He stresses that although Hegelian rational utility has infected much of the medical profession, doctors must return to older premises based on an affirmation of physicians as healers, not technicians or killers. He notes that in dealing with social problems, dictatorships can be defined as systems of thinking in destructive rather than ameliorative terms. He warns that the ease with which the destruction of life is advocated for those considered either socially useless or socially disturbing may be the first danger sign of loss of creative liberty in thinking, which is the hallmark of democratic society. The loss of educational or ameliorative potential when killing is compromised is a societal tragedy.

According to Alexander, these destructive urges cannot by definition be limited or focused on one subject or several subjects alone, but they will inevitably extend to the destroyer's entire world, including the self. Alexander effectively described the slippery slope that led from the killing of mental patients and crippled children in pre-Nazi Germany to the establishment of a lethal killing machine, which resulted in millions of innocent deaths.

Where Was the German Church?

As the killing went on in Germany, the church was strangely silent. While one of its own, Lutheran pastor Deitrich von Bonhoeffer, went to a martyr's death in a concentration camp for orchestrating a revolt against the Nazi state, mainstream churches denounced Bonhoeffer and his followers as traitors guilty of disloyalty to a "God-ordained authority." John Whitehead, in his book, *The Stealing of America*, describes the failure of the German Christians to challenge the Nazi state in opposition to the mass murders. He points out four reasons for the failure of Christians to effectively challenge Hitler:

1. The ingrained tradition of pietism—the concept that a person's private religious beliefs should be separate from the external world. This resulted in many Christians simply going about their daily lives, without their faith impacting their culture.

2. The readiness of Germans to accept the existing political order with absolute obedience to the state. Christians accepted without question the idea that the powers that be are ordained of God. They took this to mean they should not resist Hitler.

3. Many churches threw in their lot with the Nazi call for national renewal and a spiritual revival. (Many Protestant churches supported Hitler, but the Catholic church stood opposed to the dictatorship.)

4. Churchmen accepted the claim that Naziism was the only alternative to the dangers of communism.

Nazi leader Joseph Goebbels gave a clear message to the German church: "Churchmen dabbling in politics should take note that their only task is to prepare for the world hereafter."[8]

These four basic factors silenced the German church in its opposition to Hitler's mass murders.

Will the church in America continue to remain passive in the face of serious social issues facing us? Will Christians remain uninvolved in the protection of unborn children? In the protection of the handicapped, the retarded, the comatose? That answer remains to be seen.

Chapter 3

The Crisis in American Medical Ethics

The gradual conversion of German physicians from healers to killers is not merely a Nazi phenomenon. Here in the United States, it has been proceeding with increased speed over the years.

The Hegelian philosophy of rational utility is gaining ground among doctors in our country as our health care system becomes increasingly complex and expensive. Additionally, there is an aggressive secularist movement which consists of the Hemlock Society, Jack Kevorkian, and others who push their pro-death agenda in the media, through the legislatures, and in the courts.

Abortion, the killing of an unborn child, as an acceptable idea seems to be well established in the medical profession. Statistically, though, the number of abortionists is low, unlike the number of babies they kill each year, which is significant—approximately 1.5 million unborn children each year in the U.S.

The routine killing of unborn babies is viewed as a profound and sacred constitutional right by the feminists and those who profit from killing unborn children. It is accepted that abortion is a perfectly legitimate means of solving individual, social, moral, and economic problems. The baby, as was the Jewish person in Nazi Germany, is considered a nonperson, without any constitutional rights. The child who is unwanted can be killed at any time during pregnancy, for any reason, or for no reason whatsoever.

The *Roe v. Wade* and *Doe v. Bolton* cases, decided by the U.S. Supreme Court in 1973, together gave the woman an unrestricted right to kill her unborn child up to the moment of birth with physician assistance. This unrestricted access to abortion is probably the worst ethical regression that has occurred in the medical field in decades. It was a turning point in our absolute belief in the sacredness of life and the value of the individual as a person who has an inalienable right to life. These two court decisions have institutionalized killing as a form of medical care in the U.S. just as the killing of Jews and the handicapped was institutionalized in Nazi Germany. Though not approved for Germans, abortion was encouraged for non-Germans.

The philosophical underpinnings for the pro-death movement in the United States can be traced, in part, to the writings of the late Episcopal bishop and bioethicist, Joseph Fletcher. Fletcher authored *Situation Ethics* in 1966. This book, along with subsequent writings on medical ethics, provided many in the medical profession with a relativistic viewpoint of morality and of the value of human life. Fletcher was influential in providing physicians with a new criteria by which to judge life and death matters. He established what is a purely arbitrary set of guidelines to define who was a person when it came to receiving medical care. To Fletcher, *human beings* are to be distinguished from *persons*. Under Fletcher's guidelines, a person is one who has self-consciousness, sentience, brainwaves, or the ability to do complex problems. A human being, on the other hand, might not possess these capabilities and thus forfeits his constitutional protections to a right to life.

Fletcher and his so-called New Morality simply destroyed the concept of absolutes, and this relativist concept was applied to how physicians should treat their patients. Under this concept, a comatose man or woman is no longer a person because he or she fails to meet the criteria set forth for personhood. Nor does the unborn baby since it has no self-consciousness.

Fletcher's definition of personhood is inaccurate, of course, and should never have been adopted as a way of determining the value of a person. A human being should never be judged to be of greater or lesser value than another person based solely on the functions he can perform.

A man or woman who gets in a car wreck and is comatose does not cease to be a person because he or she lacks self-consciousness at that point. A person who is asleep in his bed has not ceased to be a person just because he is in a nonfunctioning state of consciousness. To separate the idea of human being from person is a philosophical atrocity which has done tremendous damage to the concept of the sanctity of human life. An unborn child is just as much a human being as the elderly man in a convalescent home.

As I said, the separating of person from human being is arbitrary and incorrect—but it serves the purposes of those determined to kill the unwanted or burdensome.

This relativistic philosophy is similar in many ways to the philosophy of Binding and Hoche in recommending the killing of persons unworthy of life. Fletcher's philosophy has been applied to justify killing deformed children, permitting and abetting suicide, and active euthanasia.

Related to Fletcher's philosophy of moral relativism is the idea of personal autonomy. The individual is the final determiner of what is right or wrong for him, and no one should intervene. If a person wishes to kill himself, he should have that right. As he wrote in his book, *To Love and to Die*, "If it is believed that the well being of persons is the highest good, then it follows that either suicide or mercy killing could be the right thing to do in some exigent and tragic circumstances."

The Fletcher view life leaves out the concept of a creator God and man created in His image. It also leads to the idea that because there is no God, there is also no transcendent meaning in life. All that matters is the here and now and how much a person can get out of life before he dies and becomes dust. With this secularist worldview, it is not difficult to justify the killing of the handicapped, the unborn, and the senile as a humane thing to do. In fact, the term "mercy killing" was used for years by those in the euthanasia movement. The term has fallen into disfavor, however, probably because the word killing is too accurate a description of what is taking place. The more popular term today is "death with dignity" or the "right to choice-in-dying." Those terms place a more positive spin on what is still the killing of a person. As in the Nazi movement, the modern day euthanasia movement depends on euphemisms to hide the fact that they recommend killing as a solution to social problems or personal dilemmas.

The New Morality and Sexual Activities

Fletcher's situation ethics has also had another devastating impact on our society in the area of sexuality. In situation ethics, there is no morality to sexuality. The New Morality has determined that the autonomous individual should be free to engage in whatever sexual proclivities he chooses, without the interference of the church or the state.

With sexual activity stripped of any moral context, the autonomous individual is almost obligated to find self-fulfillment in endless sexual encounters without regard to the problems it may cause others or society as a result. The young man unrestrained by traditional morality who has sex with multiple partners isn't burdened with the thought that he may get any one of them pregnant or pass venereal diseases on to them. He feels no obligation to the girls nor to society for the havoc he may wreak in their lives.

What is happening in the medical profession is an ongoing ideological war between the old concept of transcendent meaning and purpose in life versus the scientific materialistic view, which holds that mankind evolved and has no special meaning in the universe.

This New Morality has drastically impacted medical care and has resulted in the new ethic being embodied in laws enacted to protect the killing of the unwanted.

The New Ethic for Medicine

> The traditional Western ethic has always placed emphasis on the intrinsic worth and equal value of every human life regardless of its stage or condition. This ethic has had the blessing of the Judeo-Christian heritage and has been the basis for most of our laws and much of our social policy.... This traditional ethic is still clearly dominant, but there is much to suggest that it is being eroded at its core and may eventually be abandoned.... It will become necessary and acceptable to place relative, rather than absolute values on such things as human lives.... [3]

The new ethic being recommended is nothing more than the devaluation of human life. It is the stripping away of man's inherent dignity as a creation of God and reduces man to nothing more than a clever animal. In fact, secular ethicists like Peter Singer have actually stated that animals are superior in intelligence compared to a severely retarded person. Pigs, cows, and chickens, says Singer, have a greater capacity to relate to others, better ability to communicate, and far more curiosity, than the most severely retarded humans.

Christian bioethicist Nigel Cameron observes that the doctors who have adopted the new ethic have abandoned traditional medicine and are now practicing veterinarian medicine. Without a belief in the sacredness of life as created by God, these doctors view the patient as an animal without a soul, spirit, or eternal destiny. With such a secularist, utilitarian outlook, it is not surprising that more and more doctors are placing relative value on life.

Back in the mid-1970s, a few physicians were warning against the new ethic in medicine. One of those was Dr. Lois Lobb, then head of research on mental illness at Patton State Hospital in California. She made a frightening prediction twenty years ago which is coming true today: "I do not advocate it—but I do predict that mercy killing in some form will be a reality within the next five years. All the signposts are up. Life has lost its value."

Dr. Lobb went on to explain that our society takes death far too casually and that the medical profession is showing the same sociological symptoms Germany experienced before Hitler came along with his final solution,

> The way our sick old people and the hopelessly insane are being treated now indicates their legal execution may be the next big step.
>
> Eliminating the helpless will probably come as civil rights legislation since a recent Supreme Court ruling on abortions indicates life is no longer sacred. I imagine our mercy killing laws will begin by legalizing death with dignity. Next I see these laws being expanded to accomplish the real goal—to get rid of people who are a burden on society.[2]

Training Doctors to Accept the New Ethic

As director of pediatrics at Sacred Heart Children's Hospital in Pensacola, Florida, it was my responsibility to oversee a residency program and a critical care facility for children. During my tenure at the hospital, my staff and I began to experience what we realized were new ethical dilemmas brought on by technological advances in medicine. We were faced with decisions involving the withholding or withdrawing of care from terminally ill patients. It became obvious to me that I needed to learn more about bioethics and how other physicians were dealing with these new technologies in the care of their patients.

In 1977, I applied for and received a grant from the National Endowment for the Humanities to attend a four-week course on bioethics at Vanderbilt University in Nashville, Tennessee.

The seminar was titled "Individual Rights and the Public Good in the Treatment of Humans" and was taught by Professor John Lachs of Vanderbilt. Approximately fifty hospital administrators, physicians, nurses, and paramedics were in attendance to review modern problems in bioethics.

On the first day of this conference, we were encouraged by Professor Lachs to be open-minded about what was to be taught. We were told we should expect to change our mindset as to the practice of medicine and how we dealt with such problems as discontinuing ventilator therapy, treating handicapped newborns, etc. The professor's ethical discourse conveyed the primary message: That we should accept as, *ethical*, abortion, infanticide, condoned suicide, and euthanasia.

I was stunned at what was imparted. After the first week, I approached the professor and asked him where these new ideas came from for the practice of medicine. He handed me a copy of the *Humanist Manifesto II* and told me this was the source of the New Ethic.

I went back to my room that evening and read the manifesto from cover to cover. The *Humanist Manifesto I* is a document first drafted in 1933 by a number of Humanists, including John Dewey, the father of progressive education. The second manifesto was published in 1973 and was signed by a number of notables including Joseph Fletcher; Betty Friedan, founder of the National Organization for Women; Isaac Asimov, author; Alan F. Guttmacher, former president of Planned Parenthood; Lawrence Lader, former chairman, National Association for the Repeal of Abortion Laws; B.F. Skinner, behavioral scientist; and others.

The *Humanist Manifesto II* views traditional religious beliefs in a creator God to be an oppressive threat to the autonomy of man. In the area of sexuality and ethics, the manifesto clearly calls for freedom of all forms of sexual expression, a right to die with dignity, a right-to-suicide, and a right to abortion on demand. This, of course, would include same-sex activities and could logically be extended to sex with consenting children (as some sexologists are condoning).

The manifesto extols an atheistic philosophy which effectively denies spirituality, denigrates religious faith, and expounds a scientific materialist viewpoint.

As one who had majored in history with a minor in philosophy in undergraduate school, I was shocked to see this philosophy as the basis of the New Ethic in medicine. It was a fundamental rejection of more than four thousand years of human history and ethical belief about the special nature of mankind in a creation made by a loving God.

In the attempt to change our mindset about the ethical practice of medicine, the professor cited a number of other philosophers and their socio-economic theories dealing with ethical dilemmas. He focused on John Stuart Mill's utilitarian philosophy for the principles of making ethical medical decisions.

In explaining the process of ethical decision-making, a utilitarian ethic was espoused. The ethical analysis portrayed consisted of three basic elements: the intent, the action, and the consequences. All values being relative or subjective, the consequence became the pragmatic governing principle—the greatest good for the greatest number. Self-actualization became the goal achieved by autonomy, i.e., individual choices superseded the morality of the choice freely made.

If, for example, you abort your baby because it would be a burden to you, your right to privacy (choice) as an individual superseded any right to life of the unborn infant. The choice to kill the child may not necessarily be a pure one, but it is far better to kill the child than to bring it into the world unwanted. The consequence of self-actualization is also viewed as beneficial to the child because he won't grow up unwanted.

This, of course, is the same consequentialist philosophy that dominated Nazi Germany during the Holocaust. The ultimate objective of cleansing Germany of unwanted Jews was all that mattered. The outcome was supposedly a good one: killing an entire race of undesirables guaranteed the security of the state.

With this philosophy, it is easy to justify any action, as long as one feels it will result in a positive outcome. In the case of abortion, the decision results in the death of the infant, but the individual autonomous choice is the overarching principle.

We were taught at this seminar that morality was the chosen behavior and whatever an individual chooses (desires) to do is ethical, as long as there is no harm to others. (In abortion, of course, the baby has been dehumanized and is a nonperson, so there is no one to harm.)

Another prominent theme in this introductory bioethics seminar was the idea that human life is a continuum which starts with fetal life (nonperson), moves to a young person (qualified life), matures to an adult (fully person), declines from the adult to the aged (qualified life), then to the person who is senile, handicapped, chronically ill, comatose (nonperson).

Notice the relative value placed on human life when this life continuum is accepted as legitimate. The only stage of life where one is fully a person under Fletcher's definition is adulthood. But as soon as you become old, you're not quite human any longer, and if you become brain damaged, you're suddenly a nonperson. On the other end of the spectrum, the unborn baby is a nonperson who can be killed by the mother at will. The young person doesn't fare much better in this scenario. He ranks as only "qualified life" until he reaches adulthood.

After this seminar concluded and I'd had a chance to go over my notes, I wrote a lengthy letter back to Lachs, challenging a number of his assertions.

In that letter I wrote, in part,

> I find myself convinced that we dare not give up any more of life as a fundamental, natural right. Indeed, I am persuaded that all rights are dependent upon the recognition of the right to life. Life is not simply a condition but is *the* at least one fundamental natural Law from which all individual rights are derived or are dependent upon, including the equal right of all men to be free.
>
> The right to life is not considered an *absolute* right as we certainly suspend this right in justifying war, self-defense, and capital punishment. Yet, I find no reason whatsoever to accord a primary fundamental status to the right to freedom, since it is dependent or co-relative to the right to life. In essence, life is life, not only in *fact*, but as *value*. Without life as a fundamental natural law value, all freedom is diminished or lost. At the least, they are co-equal as natural law—the equal right of all men to life and to be free.
>
> Is there a moral consensus as well as a cost/benefit compunction to warrant legal sanctions to establish new limits to the right to life? We have evolved many new legal sanctions (laws) to limit individual freedom in the interest of the public good. Now, must we create new rules to limit individual life? Is the moral community committed to creating new rules to justify killing?
>
> Since life is not an absolute right, is medicine to proceed logically (thinking rationally) to change its criteria of care and caring on the basis of the quality of life or meaningful life? The nonperson human life has no rights and the physician proceeds (for the public good and in humanity) to carry out medical programs of humaneness and social utility, namely, abortion on demand, infanticide, euthanasia, condoned suicide, genetic engineering, etc.
>
> The euthanasia questions (allowing to die vs. killing; action vs. non-action; passive vs. active) all are subsumed in the new ethical, legal, social category of

non-person. This is precisely how the moral community justified abortion on demand, etc. The fetus is non-person human life. Engaging the feminist thrust and the 14th amendment, they declared that the right of woman to the privacy of her body supersedes any right of the fetus as a non-person. The presence of life was mute.

The key to future philosophical (ethical sphere) discourse regarding limits to life (legal sphere) is relative only, based on the quality of life to be morally, legally, and socially defined by the moral community under the *doctrine of non-person*.

The extension of this doctrine is predictable based on history, and, in particular, the Nazi experience. In pre-WWII Germany, non-person was defined for moral, legal, and social purposes. The *state* committed to assure the public good, proceeded to exercise its moral, legal, social, economic, and political right, its duty, to *relieve* nonpersons of their lives.

First, the nonpersons in the insane asylums; then the handicapped children, and, of course, the Final Solution to the Jewish problem.

I discriminated against black people in my early life because I was informed that they were non-persons. Therefore, I had a legal, moral, and social right, and duty, to keep them in their place, for the public good. . . .

I am of the persuasion that we are already experiencing the fruit of the spirit inherent in the new limits to life, e.g., abortion on demand. Specifically, a demise of interpersonal relationships and moral commitments at all levels—individual and societal. This is clearly manifest in the demise of family, as well as that accorded humane behavior. The sanctity of life as a RIGHT is crucial to sustain the moral principles and values for free activity. Yes, I feel we need desperately to maintain the emotional safeguard regarding life or suffer the loss of individual freedom to the public good.

I honestly feel that we can make much better choices—moral and ethical decisions—that will meet our needs, individually and socially. There are valid alternatives to sacrificing our fundamental rights and values. We must act in principle, not expediency, in making moral (social) choices.

Finally, I find no compelling reason to change the current criteria governing medical practice. The physician, the patient, the family, and the community are addressing these problems in an effective way. We simply do not need any more non-persons or new legal rights and duties to meet the needs of individuals and/or society. I suggest that technology and time will reduce the cost/benefit problems of diagnosis and treatment; and, that we are rapidly solving the problems of the delivery of medical services at a reasonable cost/benefit ratio. The avenues of preventative medicine are wide open. . . .

Additionally, I deeply believe that we will be much more humane as a people if we keep our emotional safeguard to life. It will prove costly not to.

Entitlement Rights

In addition to discussing the duty of doctors to accept abortion, infanticide, suicide, and euthanasia, the professor advocated universal entitlement rights to health care for every individual from birth. The theme asserted was that children and teen-agers should be entitled to receive health care without parental consent or knowledge. Who would pay for this care? The state. The discussion began with a presumption that parents do not necessarily have authority over their own children regarding health care decisions. The so-called children's rights movement of the 1970s was instrumental in pushing this notion. Again, this represents the humanistic ideal of radical autonomy which maintains that every individual—even minor children—should have entitlement rights from birth.

An outgrowth of the children's rights movement is abortion laws that prevent parents from having any say in an abortion decision. In many states, a girl can receive an abortion referral from her school-based clinic without parental consent or knowledge. It is ironic that this same girl would have to get parental permission to go on a school field trip, but she can be on an abortionist's table in mid-afternoon, and no parental consent is desired, needed, or required.

Where Are We Now?

The legal killing of the unborn child for the convenience of the mother has been established in the U.S. since 1973, and there are no signs of this so-called choice to kill the unborn being overturned any time soon.

Pro-death doctors are now turning toward legitimizing the killing of incurable patients. In the 5 November 1992 issue of *The New England Journal of Medicine*, Dr. Timothy Quill, University of Rochester School of Medicine; Dr. Christine K. Cassell, University of Chicago; and Dr. Diane Meier, Mount Sinai School of Medicine, coauthored an article entitled, "Care of the Hopelessly Ill: Proposed Clinical Criteria for Physician-Assisted Suicide."

The article uses words like dignity, comfort, and obligation in rationalizing the need for doctors to help their patients kill themselves. The authors couch their article in compassionate tones, yet what they are proposing is that doctors participate in justifiable homicide—active participation in the killing of another human being. They attempt to soften their proposal by trying to distinguish between what they view as assisted suicide as distinct from doctors who actually serve as the agent of death. What they propose is that the doctor provide the patient with whatever poisons he or she may need in order to kill *themselves*. The doctor does not do the actual killing; he only facilitates it.

According to Quill, et al, the physician who is opposed to helping his patient kill himself should be free to refuse the opportunity, but should help the patient find another, more receptive primary physician. The doctor doing the killing is supposed to make certain that the patient killed will not lose his insurance, nor will the death be investigated by a medical examiner nor will an autopsy be performed. And, say the authors, "Under no circumstances should the family's wishes and requests override those of a competent patient."[3]

This is where we are headed. Quill and his associates consider it compassionate and good medicine to help patients kill themselves. We will deal with euthanasia in a more detailed manner in chapter 7.

Chapter 4

Feminism: Killing Families

In the summer of 1977, a flyer that piqued my interest came across my desk at the children's hospital. It announced an upcoming women's conference in Orlando and listed a number of workshops on the family, feminism, and gay rights.

I took the flyer home and mentioned to my wife, Nell, that she might want to attend the conference just to see what the latest topics were about women. She looked it over, called a friend, Pat, and they drove to Orlando to see what was happening in the women's movement.

After three days, Nell and Pat came back to Pensacola shaken up by the radicalism they had observed. They witnessed something totally new and foreign to them—radical leftwing feminism in action—planning and promoting lesbianism, Marxism, and blatantly anti-family policies. Nell and Pat had been physically and verbally abused by aggressive lesbians—"butches." Lesbians controlled the agenda from beginning to end; there was no pretense that this meeting was being run on a democratic basis. The agenda had been manipulated, and no one was allowed to stand in the way of the radical feminist steamroller.

This women's meeting was designed to push passage of the federal Equal Rights Amendment that would encode into the Constitution abortion, reproductive, and gay rights, and the rejection of traditional marriage and the family.

When Nell described her frightening experience at this meeting, I lightly brushed her off, assuming she was exaggerating. Certainly, it couldn't have been *that* bad. After all, the conference was being funded by the state and federal government. They wouldn't fund something so radical. I was to be proven dead wrong.

Nell challenged me to go with her to the national women's convention scheduled that fall in Houston. I reluctantly took up the challenge and became eyewitness to a horrifying historical event: the National Women's Convention, 18-21 November 1977.

As I sat in that convention hall and watched the feminists in action, my mouth dropped open in disbelief. I was witnessing a federally funded conference run by the most radical, leftwing women I had ever seen. They were there thanks to Jimmy Carter and a Congress-approved budget of $5 million, promoting the destruction of the traditional family; advocating the redefining of sex roles; promoting gay and abortion rights; and the undermining of Judeo-Christian morality in favor of a radical egalitarian humanistic agenda.

I couldn't get over my shock when I saw little girls walking through the convention center with orange and blue check marks above their left eyes—indicating that their mothers were going to raise them to be lesbians.

The convention was completely dominated by radical lesbian women of every stripe, including the occult, professing atheists, and Marxists. In the exposition area outside of the convention hall, feminists had erected booths to promote their various causes. I was embarrassed to see the obscene materials they were selling or giving away at these booths. Some of the booths featured a variety of sex toys for lesbians; other booths featured obscene pamphlets describing perverse sexual activities. The badges and buttons worn by the radicals were equally as embarrassing and shocking to me. Some of the buttons had slogans like, "A Woman Without a Man is Like a Fish Without a Bicycle," "Mother Nature is a Lesbian," "F—— Housework," and "Out of the Closet and Into the Street." Some of the books sold were indicative of the radical and perverted nature of those attending the conference: *The Playbook for Women About Sex, Good Vibrations, The Love My Body Book,* and others.

In addition, the International Woman's Year Commission sponsored the publication of a thirty-eight-page booklet called *A Lesbian Guide,* which was co-produced by the National Commission on the Observance of International Women's Year and the National Gay Task Force.

Imagine my surprise to see the wives of three presidents proudly attending this conference. Betty Ford, Rosalynn Carter, and Lady Bird Johnson were there to lend their support to this federally funded obscenity.

The IWY Conference in Houston was clearly a preplanned and staged media event to garner support for the radical feminist agenda. As in the Orlando conference, there was no pretense of observing parliamentary procedure in amending proposals set forth. Pro-family representatives at the conference were in a clear minority. According to Phyllis Schlafly, only 20 percent of the two thousand delegates were committed to traditional values, and they were effectively silenced by the strong-arm tactics of the feminists in charge.

The pro-family delegation was not allowed to challenge the radical resolutions being proposed, nor were they allowed to submit a minority report in protest. According to Schlafly, during three days of sessions, pro-family delegates were allowed only one one-minute statement against the ERA and two two-minute statements against abortion. No pro-family delegate was allowed to speak against federal child care legislation or lesbian rights.

As Phyllis Schafly noted in her post-conference analysis, "What Really Happened in Houston," the entire conference was a set-up from beginning to end. The International Woman's Year resolutions had been written up and published in a book, *To Form a More Perfect Union*, back in 1976. The conference was a $5 million extravaganza to simply rubber-stamp what had been determined a year before.[1]

A 25-Point Plan to Destroy Families

The IWY convention was designed by the feminists to pass a National Plan of Action, which included twenty-five demands upon the federal government. Basically, the plan was a feminist/lesbian/Marxist agenda for destroying the traditional family.

The National Plan of Action consisted of a number of proposals including:

1. The federal government should assume a major role in directing and providing comprehensive voluntary, flexible hour, bias-free, non-sexist, quality child care and developmental programs, including child care facilities for federal employees, and should request and support adequate legislation and funding for these programs.

2. State school systems should move against sex stereotyping through appropriate action.

3. The Equal Rights Amendment should be ratified.

4. We support the U.S. Supreme Court decisions which guarantee reproductive freedom to women. . . . Particular attention should be paid at all levels of government to provide confidential family planning services for teenagers, education in responsible sexuality, and reform of laws discriminating against illegitimate children and their parents.

5. Congress, state, and local legislatures should enact legislation to eliminate discrimination on the basis of sexual and affectional preference in areas including, but not limited to, employment, housing, public accommodations, credit, public facilities, government funding, and the military.

6. As part of the president's proposed government reorganization plan, Congress and the president should establish a cabinet-level women's department in the executive branch of the federal government to help insure

that all persons are guaranteed equal opportunities without regard to sex.[2]

A Pro-Family Counter-Convention

Fortunately for Nell and I, we didn't leave this convention totally disillusioned about the future of our country and the family. We were to discover that a counter-convention was taking place across town as a protest to the feminist-dominated IWY meeting. The counter-convention had been organized by Phyllis Schlafly and a number of other pro-family leaders to present a genuinely pro-family, pro-moral opposition to the IWY fiasco.

We attended the pro-family gathering and were surprised to find ourselves in the midst of fifteen thousand men and women who were firmly committed to God, country, and family. This conference had been privately funded, and every person attending had paid his or her own way to be there. It was encouraging to both of us to see the great outpouring of love and concern for the traditional family and Judeo-Christian morality. There were dozens of groups represented at this convention including STOP ERA, Eagle Forum, Conservative Caucus, National Right to Life, March for Life, National Council of Catholic Women, Daughters of the American Revolution, and others.

The contrast between the two conventions was astonishing to us. I was dismayed by the lack of media coverage for the pro-family convention, which had an attendance four times as large as the IWY convention. However, it was barely mentioned in the Houston press while we were there. The IWY conference, on the other hand, was given daily, slanted, favorable coverage in newspapers and on TV and radio.

As I watched the biased coverage given to the IWY conference compared to the pro-family convention, I lost my naivete concerning the press. It was obvious to us that the media was actively promoting the radical feminist agenda and ignoring or ridiculing the pro-family movement.

Changed Lives, Changed Directions

Nell, Pat, and I were forever changed by our experiences in Houston at the IWY conference and the pro-family convention. We realized that something very serious and threatening was happening to our nation. We had come face to face with a radical socio-political movement that was intolerant of opposition and extremely aggressive in pursuing its vision for our government and social systems, including the demise of the traditional family. I became acutely aware of the dangers that feminism would pose for the future welfare of our children and teen-agers. They were very clear about their plan to destroy what they considered a patriarchal family structure which placed the male as the head of the nuclear family.

In fact, as their writings show, they considered any male-dominated institution as worthy of destruction, including what they envisioned was a male-dominated view of reality. Feminist writer Ruth Bleier, once wrote: "Truth, reality, and objectivity are all in trouble from our point of view; we see a male-created truth and reality, a male point of view, a male-defined objectivity."[3]

It was feminist writer Betty Friedan, later founder of NOW and signer of the *Humanist Manifesto II* in 1973, who launched the current feminist revolution with her book, *The Feminine Mystique*, in 1963. In this analysis of the role of wives and mothers, Friedan described the traditional family as an institution that represses and enslaves women. She compared homemakers to parasites and said that sexist ideas were burying millions of American women alive.

Women, said Friedan, could only become fully liberated when they entered the work force and attained equality with men in the business world. They were also to be as sexually liberated as men; thus the push for promiscuous sex, birth control, and abortion as means of disposing of the unwanted children who might be conceived as a result of this liberation.

In 1970, feminist author Germaine Greer contributed more revolutionary rhetoric to help destroy the traditional family by writing *The Female Eunuch*. In her view, motherhood is a handicap, and pregnancy is an illness. She urged women to be deliberately promiscuous and then attacked the institution of marriage with these words, "If women are to effect a significant amelioration in their condition, it seems obvious that they must refuse to marry."[5]

Betty Friedan, Germaine Greer, and a host of other radical feminist thinkers spewed out volumes of anti-family books in an effort to destroy the patriarchal two-parent family. Unfortunately, their ideas have so permeated our culture that they have succeeded in destroying millions of marriages and in the process have brought untold social destruction to our culture.

Getting Involved in the Pro-family Movement

Once back in Pensacola, Nell and I immediately got involved in conservative, Christian organizations seeking to actively oppose the feminist agenda. Nell became a leading spokeswoman for a group called Women for Responsible Legislation. She began writing, travelling throughout the state, and speaking to women's groups on the dangers of the Equal Rights Amendment and radical feminism. She joined Eagle Forum and worked closely with Phyllis Schafly and other pro-family women in Florida to help defeat the ERA. Nell developed a friendship with Eliza Paschal, the former national secretary of the National Organization for Women, who had become disillusioned by the extremely radical agenda of the feminist movement. Nell and Eliza became co-speakers, travelling the state to fight passage of the ERA. Their efforts, along with other pro-family women, helped in the eventual defeat of the ERA in our state—and ultimately led to the defeat of the ERA nationally.

The ERA was one of the most radical, yet deceptive, proposals to be offered by the feminists. If passed, it would have federalized all child and family law and removed any state authority in dealing with family issues. The federal government would have been given unprecedented power to restructure family life, to redefine the family, to abolish any distinctions between males and females in our laws, to legalize lesbian relationships, and more.

In opposing the ERA, Nell gave numerous speeches to civic groups and churches. In one of her speeches she accurately described the ultimate effect of the ERA with these words:

> The Equal Rights Amendment mandates that the laws of the land forget the outmoded concept of two sexes. All laws, civil or criminal, must be genderless—and this means any differentiation in the legal treatment on the basis of sex is not permissible—for any reason whatsoever—no matter how reasonable.
>
> The second section of this proposed amendment says, "Congress shall have the power to enforce by appropriate legislation, the provisions of this article." Now listen carefully to this, as most people do not realize the impact of this section.
>
> In the *Katzenbach v. Morgan* Supreme Court case, the court ruled that if a constitutional amendment contains a clause giving Congress the power to enforce by appropriate legislation, then Congress can preempt the field and the states lose jurisdiction to legislate on that subject.
>
> You know that this means Congress would pass the legislation; the Supreme Court would interpret it; and the federal bureaus would make the rules and administer them.
>
> In effect, this would remove to the federal level all laws regarding marriage, divorce, child custody, inheritance, property laws, and all other laws involving men and women. Any objections to laws defining people by sex would be resolved by appointed judges answerable to no one, not by our elected officials

who answer to the electorate. This would, in the end, make the states merely administrators of the federal laws—and would mean a rule of the minority instead of the majority. This is a rip off of states' rights and a denial of our system of federalism, which is the envy of the world!

Nell went on to describe portions of the twenty-five-point plan presented at the IWY convention and then explained the feminist philosophy by quoting from a number of feminist sources, including *Document: A Declaration of Feminism*, presented at a feminist conference in Minneapolis, Minnesota, in January, 1972. The document says in part:

> Heterosexual relationships are by their very nature oppressive to women in a male-dominated society.
>
> Marriage has existed for the benefit of men and has been a legally sanctioned method of control over women.
>
> That the nuclear family has been particularly isolating to women. The nuclear family must be replaced with a new form of family, where individuals live and work together to help meet the needs of all people in the society.

Nell ended her speech with an appeal to her audience to reject the ERA:

> Our nation is not embroiled in a battle of sexes, but a battle of philosophies—between those in our camp who hold the pro-family, traditional, biblical views upon which our nation was founded, and those of the opposing side who embrace the humanist-feminist philosophy—and advocate, ultimately, the end of our system of Western Culture.
>
> If our children have no strong family ties, no strong gender identity, conflicting sexual orientation—how can they be positive males or females? How can they nurture families of their own?

I propose to you that these feminists, or radical women liberationists, do not speak for the majority of American women. Most of us are concerned with our families, our children, our homes, drugs among our young people, pornography—especially the horrendous child pornography, crime—and in particular the crime of rape, high taxes; and very high on our list is the education our youngsters are receiving.

For too long the feminists have tried to make you believe that the current women's movement is none of men's business. Nothing could be more false! Everything involved in this movement is going to affect men very directly. It is going to affect your wives, daughters, grandchildren, and the entire social structure in which men live. Men—it *is* your business! We of the pro-family movement are begging you to step forward and let your voices be heard—loud and clear—in Tallahassee and Washington!

We can stop this destructive trend by getting moral men and women registered as voters—then to make sure they get to the polls on election day—and to vote only God-fearing, family, caring men into office!

Do you remember God destroyed Sodom because He couldn't find ten righteous men? I believe if enough godly men and women stand up for their beliefs, we will not be destroyed by these evil forces. I, for one, will be counted!

Of course, Nell's work—and the work of dozens of other pro-family women paid off—and the ERA was eventually defeated. Unfortunately, many of the objectives of the feminists have since been accomplished year by year through changes in laws and through court decisions which have undermined the stability of the family.

Family: Our Responsibility

As Nell travelled throughout Florida fighting feminism and the ERA, I decided to tackle the feminist threat in another way. I founded a citizens group called Family

Our Responsibility (FOR). Its purpose was to educate Floridians as to the value of the traditional two-parent family—the most important social unit in society. As I studied family issues, it became more and more obvious to me that the nuclear family, with a father, mother, and children, was the basic building block of civilization. The family is the place where our children are nurtured and where values are transmitted; it is the place where morality is taught and where children are civilized and prepared for life as adults.

I held the first meeting of FOR on 23 January 1978 and began to develop a number of seminars on the importance of the family. In April of 1979, I worked in cooperation with the Institute for Pediatric Service and the children's medical center at Sacred Heart Hospital in Pensacola to sponsor a major symposium on the family. Keynote speakers were such notables as Dr. Amitai Etzioni, Director and Professor of Sociology at Columbia University; Dr. Bruce Graham, Professor of Pediatrics from Ohio State University; Dr. Steven Sawchuk, Chairman of the Board, Institute for Pediatric Service and Director of Medical Services, Johnson & Johnson Baby Products Company, and others.

Etzioni gave an excellent keynote speech, "Can We Do Without a Traditional Family," and the conference ended with a panel discussion on the importance of the nuclear family.

During the years I headed FOR, I spoke a number of times on family breakdown to civic groups and churches. In one of those speeches, I noted that our future does not depend primarily on technology, or the environment, but on the kind of people we are. In turn, the kind of people of each generation depends on the competence and character of our children, i.e., their abilities and values. The kind of people our children will become is determined by their nurture and care—the role and function of the family. Therefore, the family is the key to our future.

I went on to explain that I could see multiple factors

which were contributing to the breakdown of the traditional family: divorce, desertion, mobility and a radical sexual, humanist and feminist revolution during the sixties and seventies. Additional factors were simply offshoots of the radicalism that occurred just prior to and following the Vietnam War protests: the gay rights movement; the revolution in medical ethics which promoted abortion on demand, infanticide, and euthanasia; the revolution in family law which included children's liberation, the growth of federal bureaucracies, and the centralization of government; a changing work ethic which placed more value on hedonism than productivity; and the expansion of the media's role as opinion-molder, rather than objective reporter of the news.

The family, of course, is the first and best department of health, education, and welfare for its members. It is the vital center for human development, and its role is absolutely essential in transmitting values to children. Dr. Harold Voth, a psychiatrist and expert on family issues, says the family is vital for developing in the child human qualities of trust and love and bonds of affection that reduce the potential for children to suffer disorders of non-attachment. The family provides the primary source of moral authority which forms a stable and principled identity for the child's character and personality.[6]

The Men Rebelled First

Unfortunately, the feminists, along with the followers of Hugh Hefner's Playboy philosophy, have been most responsible for the destruction of the traditional family and the stability it provides for children and for husbands and wives to exist in a loving, nurturing environment.

If you take a look at the history of pornography and feminism during the past forty years, it is sad to note that Hugh Hefner set off a revolution among men that is still causing social destruction among families. Hefner's Playboy philosophy was very simple: it glorified uncommitted relationships between men and women; it promoted unrestrained sexual promiscuity and eagerly promoted abortion, birth control, and the supposed sexual equality between men and women.

With millions of men buying into Hefner's philosophy, it became commonplace for men to drift from one sexual liaison to another without any hint of commitment or love; with relaxed divorce laws, it became routine for married men to desert their wives when a younger centerfold came along. After all, Hugh Hefner was the role model. As he aged, his playmates always remained young and sexually available. Why shouldn't the sophisticated reader of *Playboy* always have access to young women—without the inconvenience of marriage or children?[7]

Both feminists and playboys contributed to the destruction of the traditional family. And both were closely linked to the secular humanist revolution which swept through every social institution of our society during the sixties and seventies.

Radical Feminism Kills Family Stability

The feminist philosophy is most obviously evident in the pro-abortion movement in this country. The feminist ideology has managed to protect the so-called right to abortion, and the killing of unborn babies remains largely unrestricted in this country. The feminist ideology has also been effective in putting a wedge between teen-agers and their parents by prohibiting the passage of parental notification or parental consent laws.

In the medical field, I have noticed the influence of feminism evident in our professional associations. Professional groups such as the American Academy of Pediatrics are basically liberal in their orientation and tend to support the feminist agenda. Large numbers of women who work in the medical field subscribe to the feminist philosophy, and they have great influence in setting the policies and practices of medical societies, hospitals, and foundations which distribute medical research grants.

Organizations like the American Medical Association (AMA) and the American Academy of Pediatrics (AAP) seem to be dominated by the feminist viewpoint. They have undue influence on medical policies, task forces, in committees, and in academic settings. The result of this influence is children's liberation policy that views parents as incapable of properly caring for children; that views the professionals as better equipped to nurture children; that diminishes parental authority and places ultimate authority in the state.

In the social arena, the feminist movement has contributed significantly to the destruction of the traditional family—and has directly contributed to the decline in the general well-being of our children and teen-agers—because of broken families.

The Divorce Choice

The feminist-inspired idea of no-fault divorce that gained popularity back in the 1970s has brought about the feminization of poverty because it has made it far too easy for a family to suffer divorce, resulting in the wife's diminished income and support. Until the 1960s and 1970s, traditional divorce laws were designed to make it difficult for families especially with children, to split apart. There had to be adultery or brutality involved in order for the couples to split. With the no-fault divorce concept, however, only one party had to assert an irretrievable breakdown in the relationship.

The feminists thought that no-fault divorce would liberate women from the oppression of men. What it has done is liberate men from their responsibilities as husbands and fathers and has plunged freedom-seeking women and their children into poverty and despair.

The Family Research Council issued a report not long ago that describes the terrible results of easy divorce on women and children. Easy divorce affects not only their economic well-being, but their psychological and physical well-being.

According to the FRC report, *Free to be Family*, easy divorce has been a disaster—especially for children. "Children of divorce typically experience depression, slackened school performance, episodic drug and alcohol use, and a diminished ability to form lasting relationships. Thus divorce feeds upon itself, each generation producing a new one less apt to form enduring marriages."[8]

The report notes that the number of children affected by divorce has increased from 300,000 in 1950 to more than 1.04 million in 1988.

The no-fault divorce revolution directly affected the economic well-being of women with children. This revolution began in California in 1970 as a way of overcoming drawn-out conflicts in divorce proceedings. A similar law was passed soon afterward in Florida and spread rapidly throughout the U.S.

Under no-fault divorce, only one partner was needed to dissolve the marriage on the flimsiest of excuses. It was an anomaly in American law because it became easier to divorce than to break any other kind of binding contract involving two or more parties. The feminists viewed no-fault divorce as a way of becoming liberated from male domination. It certainly liberated the man from any enforceable financial responsibility to pay alimony; he was usually only required to pay child support—which was seldom accomplished.

Children were the ones most victimized by no-fault divorce. They and their mother routinely ended up in poverty because the ex-husband would refuse to pay child support and would often flee the state to avoid paying anything.

As a result of no-fault divorce, we have seen a dramatic surge in the number of single-parent families, headed by women and plunged into poverty. The feminization of poverty is a very real consequence of a feminist-inspired law.

The statistics on single-parent homes are frightening and signal a further breakdown of our society in the years ahead as children from these broken homes become adults. According to the FRC's *Free to be Family*, "27.1 percent of our nation's children are born into single-parent homes; in the black community, this figure is 68 percent. The number of children in single-female-headed homes has increased 170 percent, rising from 5.1 million in 1960 to 13.7 million in 1989."[9]

The destruction of the two-parent family means hardship, poverty, and despair for millions of women and children. It means increased welfare dependency and increased remedial educational needs for children of single-parent homes. It means increased incidences of crime by delinquent children from single-parent homes. It means increasing incidences of pregnancy of girls who come from single-parent homes, and it means a general decline in the entire well-being of our culture.

There are literally hundreds of studies which prove conclusively that children from single-parent homes are at risk socially, psychologically, physically, and spiritually. The absence of a father for a boy often results in greatly increased incidences of juvenile delinquency. A 1988 study published in the *Journal of Research on Crime and Delinquency*, for example, found that the proportion of single-parent families in a community is the best predictor of violent crime and burglary in a city—not poverty.[10]

As a matter of fact, it is virtually impossible for a single mother to control a young male who is acting out his anger. Without the partnership of two parents—and especially a strong father—it is nearly inevitable that young males of single mothers will fail in some way. They will either fail educationally or socially by committing crimes. (This is not inevitable if the single mother and her children have a strong religious commitment and have found appropriate male role models in church.)

Dr. George Rekers, a clinical psychologist and professor at the University of South Carolina, is an expert on the impact that the absence of fathers can have on boys and girls. He writes:

> The absence of the father for boys has been linked to greater occurrences of effeminacy, higher dependence, less successful adult heterosexual adjustment, greater aggressiveness or exaggerated masculine behavior. . . . In girls, . . . compared with girls with intact nuclear families, girls who lost their father by death were more inhibited in their relationships with males in general, but girls who lost their fathers by divorce were overly responsive to males, were more likely to be sexually involved with males in adolescence, married younger, were pregnant more often before marriage, and became divorced or separated from their eventual husbands more frequently.[11]

As I have worked with children and teen-agers during the past forty years, I can attest to the accuracy of these statistics and statements. During part of my career as a pediatrician, I volunteered time to work with teen-agers held in detention centers in Pensacola. Between 1970 and 1980, I noticed a frightening change in the behavior and attitudes of these youngsters. In the seventies, these youngsters were sullen and often uncooperative, but they didn't exhibit the incredibly violent anger that the teens in the eighties exhibited. In a ten-year period, teens held in detention became extremely violent, vicious with each other and with anyone attempting to help them. Our attendants had to wear rubber mouth pieces in order to avoid having their teeth knocked out by violent and unrepentant teens. I noticed the same trend among girls who were held in detention centers. They had become just as violent and uncontrollable as their male counterparts.

In working with community mental health centers and psychologists attempting to rehabilitate these youngsters, I became all too familiar with their family backgrounds. I can say with accuracy that 85 to 90 percent of these teens were victims of broken homes. These young people evidenced much despair and anger because of their family instability, and scores of them turned to drugs and alcohol for escape. This, of course, just exacerbated their condition and altered their behavior toward even more violent behavior. These unfortunate kids couldn't concentrate, couldn't learn, and couldn't control their behaviors.

At the children's hospital, I often experienced a great deal of frustration in treating youngsters from single-parent homes. I literally spent half of my time working in consultation with social workers to make sure that these children would be returned for check-ups and would receive proper medication at home. Quite often the single mother just didn't have the personal discipline necessary to make sure her child received follow-up care through our hospital clinics.

I can remember my frustration sitting in public program planning meetings and listening to the experts discuss all of the new programs that they were going to devise or seek government funding for to cope with the effects of broken families. I would often attempt to bring up the importance of the two-parent family as a solution to many of our social problems, but any talk of two-parent families was considered judgmental of single parents. It was considered offensive to moralize about the value of husbands and wives. It seemed more important for the social planners to consider everyone a victim and to create new bureaucracies to deal with societal breakdown. I might add that the only person in the equation who wasn't considered a victim or treated with kid gloves was the absent father. He was routinely blamed for everything—but no one seemed willing to consider attempts to restore broken relationships or prevent them from becoming broken.

The Adolescent Health Crisis

The feminist- and playboy-inspired sexual revolution has brought about a devastating epidemic of venereal diseases among teen-agers. Dr. Joe McIlhaney, writing in *Sexuality and Sexually Transmitted Diseases*, points out the following grim facts:

- 30 percent of single, sexually active Americans have herpes.

- 30 percent of single, sexually active young adults have Venereal Wart Virus, which can cause cervical cancer and cancer of the penis in men.

- 30-40 percent of sexually active Americans have chlamydia, which can often result in sterility for women.

- 16 out of every 100,000 Americans have syphilis.[12]

The Family Research Council (FRC) reports that 63 percent of sexually transmitted diseases occur among people under the age of twenty-five. FRC notes that twenty-seven thousand new cases of venereal disease occur every day in the United States and that syphilis has reached its highest level since 1950 with forty-eight thousand new cases reported in 1990.[13]

FRC also reports that as many as 100,000 women are made sterile by gonorrhea each year, while 6 percent of women who have just one episode of gonococcal pelvic inflammatory disease will become sterile.[14]

According to FRC's *Free to be Family*,

> The fertility of teenage women is in particular jeopardy. Sexually experienced teens are 1.7 times more likely than sexually experienced 25-29 year-olds to be diagnosed with PID, primarily caused by chlamydia or gonorrhea. In 1988, 210,000 women were hospitalized for PID; 43% were under 25. Of those hospitalized women, 29,000 required hysterectomies.[15]

Teen suicide is also hitting epidemic proportions—largely due to drug abuse and the breakdown of the traditional two-parent family. The suicide rate has increased 300 percent since 1950 for teen-agers—and 50 percent of suicidal youth come from single parent homes. According to Harvard psychiatrist Dr. Armand M. Nicholi, "An overview of recent research in the field points—with unmistakable clarity—to the changes in child-rearing practices and in the stability of the home as significant factors in the rapidly rising rate of suicide."[16]

Of course, with Hemlock Society founder Derek Humphry lobbying hard to have suicide legalized and institutionalized, we should not be surprised to see an even greater incidence of suicide among teens in the future.

The promotion of suicide as a right has been aided in recent years by University of California psychiatrist Dr. Jerome A. Motto, whose essay, *Suicide is an Individual Right*, is disseminated in public schools through the textbook, *Problems of Death: Opposing Viewpoints*. In his essay, Motto says, "The question as to whether a person has the right to cope with the pain in his world by killing himself can be answered without hesitation: He does have that right."[17]

Clearly, the humanistic notions of radical individualism and autonomy have impacted the medical profession's response to adolescent health care issues.

As a former member of the bioethics committee of the American Academy of Pediatrics, I attempted to get the committee to endorse a resolution condemning condoned suicide. My resolution was never passed. A majority of the members of the bioethics committee at that time seemed to sanction the idea that individuals have a right to kill themselves if they choose.

Children's Rights Invade the Medical Profession

Linked very closely with the feminist ideology of radical autonomy is the children's rights movement, which has also had a detrimental effect on family stability and parental rights. The children's rights advocates—represented by such organizations as the Children's Defense Fund—view parents as little more than caretakers for state property. First Lady Hillary Clinton, of course, has been active for years in the CDF, as well as her friend and confidant, Donna Shalala, the new head of the Department of Health and Human Services, overseeing the surgeon general's office and our public health system.

Child advocates in the social welfare system and in our medical system are continually pushing for legislation and court rulings which will liberate children and adolescents from the control of their parents. This effort to liberate children has been very successful in the area of abortion, where most states do not allow parents to be consulted when their adolescent daughters seek abortions.

The American Academy of Pediatrics, unfortunately, has been a leader in promoting the idea that children are entitled to health care as a basic right—without parental knowledge or consent. An AAP policy adopted in 1990 maintains that "pediatricians should be free to counsel teen-age patients about sexual behavior, contraceptives, prevention of STDs, and access to family planning services without parental consent or knowledge and in a non-judgmental, non-threatening environment in which a teen can acknowledge sexual concerns and experiences."[18]

The old paradigm in medicine, when dealing with teen-agers, assumed that the parent would have final authority over the medical care of the child. The doctor was to go through the parent to treat the child. Under the new paradigm, the parent is nearly irrelevant in the process. The doctor is to feel free to deal directly with the teen-ager and has no obligation to consult the parent—unless he chooses to do so with the assent or consent of the adolescent.

The truth of the matter is that medical issues involving teens quite often lead to potential injuries due to a pregnancy, prescribed forms of contraception, abortion, drug abuse, and attempted suicide. It would seem only prudent for the physician to seek parental involvement in these issues—especially when the parent will be held responsible for whatever medical costs are involved. In my opinion, the physician, acting in the best interest of the adolescent, should actively involve the parent in the decision-making process, to assure active intervention and long-term resolution of high risk behavior.

In a proposal to the AAP, I suggested that the academy adopt a resolution which would urge doctors to negotiate an oral contract with parents and adolescents prior to giving health services. This agreement would be applicable to public and private practices under responsible professional supervision.

I listed the principles of this physician/parent/adolescent agreement as follows:

1. Parental consent and notification is in the best interest of the adolescent when the parent(s)/family are available and functioning. Therefore, the pediatrician should maintain the right of parental consent and notification, preferably, but not necessarily, with the adolescent's assent.

2. Parental consent and notification is not in the best interest of the adolescent when there is parent(s)/family failure or the adolescent is emancipated for specific reasons of law. Thus, exceptions to the general principle of parental consent and notification may be justified by a reasonable, responsible exercise of the physician's judgment in the best interest of the adolescent.

3. Assuming available and functioning parent(s)/family, the specifics of this agreement are as follows:

   A. Sexual abstinence is commended as the ideal for the adolescent.

   B. Non-prescriptive, publicly available barrier/chemical methods of contraception are safe, effective, inexpensive, accessible, readily utilized, and afford adequate contraception when abstinence is rejected. Parental consent and/or confidentiality are not at issue.

   C. Prescribed contraception, i.e., the IUD and the pill, and abortion involve potential serious harm and risk for the adolescent, and therefore warrant parental consent and notification.

   D. The management of substance abuse in the adolescent is peculiarly dependent upon parent(s)/family involvement and warrants parental notification.

E. The treatment of venereal disease is a pragmatic need and, as a public health interest, warrants confidentiality or adolescent assent to parental notification.

F. Conversely, in the circumstance of parent(s)/family failure, the physician may proceed with informed consent of the adolescent and act in the best interest of the adolescent as follows:

Abstinence remains a suitable ideal to be preferred. Barrier/chemical contraception is counselled. Prescribed contraception, i.e., the IUD and the pill, is an option which involves potential for serious harm and risk that does require consent and warrants parent(s)/family notification and consent.

This resolution was never accepted—primarily because it involved parents in medical decisions involving adolescents.

Restoring the Two-Parent Family

In the last few pages we have dealt with a number of issues that have contributed to the destruction of the two-parent family. Our tremendously complex social problems involving sexuality, delinquency, drug dependency, etc., can all be significantly reduced if we would acknowledge the fact that the two-parent family is the only way we can bring order out of the chaos that has resulted from the sexual revolution, radical feminism, liberal media influence, and an aggressive secular humanism movement in our country.

There is simply no valid alternative to the two-parent family—yet our social engineers naively think they can create new social organizations and programs that will provide the same kind of nurturing environment that the two-parent family provides. They are dead wrong. History proves them wrong, and our current social pathology proves them wrong.

Our current social policies are bankrupt and must be replaced with policies which acknowledge that the two-parent family is the ideal social organization in which to bring up children. Unfortunately, with radical feminists and humanists dominating government, academia, and the medical profession, it will take a great effort to bring us *back* to the two-parent family and stable, peaceful homes.

We desperately need to return to the much maligned "Ozzie and Harriet" days when children were taught the basic, timeless truths about honesty, self-discipline, chastity, and patriotism. The feminists ridicule the 1950s with its image of "Ozzie and Harriet" and "Father Knows Best" TV programs, but as one who brought up children during that period, it was a wonderful, peaceful time.

We need to return to those days when the streets were safe, when there were caring neighbors and where it was taken for granted that marriage was for life. We should return to those days when our social institutions supported traditional Judeo-Christian morality and we had few social pathologies to confront us.

Of course, the feminists decry the 1950s as the dark ages of slavery for women because it was assumed that the home would be headed by a male. In their largely successful efforts to destabilize the male-dominated two-parent family, the feminists have helped introduce serious social pathologies into our culture—pathologies that will take generations to heal. One of their greatest successes is in legalizing the killing of unborn children. Fortunately, they were not so successful in helping legalize infanticide back in the early 1980s.

Chapter 5

Killing the Unborn

In Wichita, Kansas, Dr. George Tiller operates Women's Health Care Services. The clinic name sounds innocuous enough. One would suppose that this physician is involved in providing compassionate care for women with physical problems. The name of this clinic, however, is as misleading as the names the Nazis gave to their death camps and forced relocation programs.

Dr. George Tiller, nicknamed "Tiller the Killer" by Wichita pro-lifers, is engaged in the lucrative business of killing second and often third trimester babies.

Tiller's promotional brochure says that only abnormal fetuses are candidates for his Fetal Indications Program, but a former Tiller employee has revealed that his program also includes healthy babies as candidates for extermination.

Tiller's promotional brochure puts a positive spin on the killing of late term babies. Under the clinic's purpose statement, we read,

> Our purpose at Women's Health Care Services is to guide and support women through an experience which will allow them the opportunity to change the rest of their lives.
>
> We are here to help our patients make their DREAMS COME TRUE by maximizing their assets and minimizing their shortcomings.

> We are dedicated to providing the chance for women to live joyous, productive and free lives. The cornerstones of our organization are Attitude, Team Care, Safety and Comfort. We are a Recovery-based institution.

How does Tiller help women's dreams to come true? According to a former Tiller employee,

> The first day the procedure is initiated, a needle is inserted into the living heart of the fetus and a feticidal agent, as Dr. Tiller calls it, is injected to kill the fetus.
>
> Over the next couple of days, laminaria packs are inserted into the cervix of the patient, and labor-inducing drugs are administered. Sonograms are done at various points in the procedure—and Dr. Tiller measures the BPD (bi-parietal diameter) at its narrowest point, instead of at the usually measured widest point, leading to a BPD reading by Dr. Tiller of, say, 24 weeks gestation, when the accepted norm might be 26 weeks gestation—however, this method is not illegal, but is currently just a matter of accepted practice.
>
> Aided by the body's natural inclination to expel a dead fetus, labor commences on the 4th or 5th day, and the group of patients are kept in a room in the basement together, separated by only a few feet of space from each other, and delivered of their dead infants. However, occasionally a labor begins at the motel where the patients are required to stay, so Dr. Tiller keeps a nurse there at night. . . .

According to this former employee, who worked with Tiller's medical records, he performs an average of ten to twenty late-term abortions each week. "Through that information, and by figuring a conservatively high cost-of-doing business, I estimate that Dr. Tiller's entire practice, consisting primarily of the late-term abortions, brings in a net of $500,000 per year, in addition to his investments and other ventures."

After killing the late-term child, Tiller offers a "Fetal Indications Support and Healing Group" for those women and husbands who are having difficulty coping with the death of their child. According to a letter written by Tiller to an OB/GYN doctor in April of 1991,

> All possible efforts are made to allow the patient's husband/spousal alternative to accompany the patient through the labor and miscarriage process.
>
> They are encouraged to be involved in our Fetal Indications Identification and Separation Encounter. In this encounter they are introduced to the normal features of their baby as well as the anomalies. Patients are encouraged to speak directly to their baby if they wish, and finally, to say good-bye. (Not all patients choose to be involved in this process but we feel that this encounter facilitates the natural process of releasing, letting-go and saying good-bye.) . . .
>
> The patient may elect to receive fetal ashes. Fetal photographs and a report are mailed to the referring physician.

Tiller, of course, has his own crematoria on the premises to efficiently dispose of the bodies of these unwanted children. The smoke which rises from his crematoria is a grim reminder of Auschwitz and other Nazi death camps where the same services were rendered to Jews and other enemies of the Nazi state.

Dr. Tiller's enterprise is only a symptom of the serious moral and ethical crisis which exists in our society today impacting the medical profession.

The Story of Baby David

Chad Traywick of Houston, Texas, learned first-hand what happens inside an abortion clinic. Chad became involved in pro-life work in September of 1989. Three months later, he was to find himself involved in a bizarre episode involving an aborted baby, a police SWAT team, and more publicity than he had ever imagined.

On 9 December 1989, Chad was returning to Houston from Austin where he was visiting his sister-in-law who had been jailed for Operation Rescue activities. As he was driving home, he felt that he needed to be more active in pro-life activities in his own community.

That afternoon, he decided to find the closest abortion clinic near his house so he could begin picketing it on a regular basis with his wife. When he arrived at the clinic, he noticed that Women's Pavilion, as it was called, was housed in a four-story building. He wasn't sure which side of the abortion clinic faced the area where he would be picketing, so he went inside to find the office.

To his surprise, the building was unlocked; there were no security guards in the lobby, and no surveillance camera was evident. He found the clinic office on the fourth floor and noticed the clinic windows faced the back of the building instead of the front where he was going to picket. Before he left, he thought he would introduce himself and tell the clinic receptionist that the abortionist could expect pickets outside of his office every weekend. When he poked his head inside the clinic door, he was surprised to find the office empty. Since he had never been in an abortion clinic before, he thought he would take a look around.

After walking through a plush reception area, he noted a small room with what looked like a steam vat in it. Beside this vat were stacks of medical instruments. As he turned to leave the room, he noticed a row of plastic containers on the floor against the wall. He leaned over to examine the containers and noticed umbilical cords floating near the top. He knew immediately that these butter-bowl-like containers held the remains of aborted babies. In a quick decision, he took one of the containers with the date, 8 December 1989, written on the lid and some forceps—as evidence that he had taken the items from an abortion clinic.

He left the building quickly, not knowing exactly what he was going to do with this aborted child; but he knew something significant had happened that afternoon.

He decided to take photographs of the baby, as it was laid out on his kitchen table. As he peeled back the lid, he found the container full of blood mixed with a preservative of some kind. The baby's head was floating near the top, with the body of the child curled around the inside of the container. The baby's head was big as a softball, indicating it was either a second or third trimester child.

As Chad tells the story,

> I then reached for his body and began to lift it out. It seemed as though it would not stop coming! I had to use both hands to hold him. He was at least a foot long! I knew right away that this was no second trimester child, but that he was almost full term!
>
> We judged him at first to be at least six months, then later we figured at least seven months. It has since been guessed by a doctor and other pro-life people who have had similar experiences that he may have been eight months. Either way, he was very far along—he was later measured at full sixteen inches and weighed about three pounds.
>
> The umbilical cord and placenta were still attached. An intentional incision had been made in his back and organs removed—probably his kidney or pancreas. We also found no trace of his brain.

Chad theorizes that the abortionist may have sold these body organs for research or transplant purposes.

The Photos and a Police Encounter

Chad and some friends took photographs and a lengthy video of the baby as evidence of the killing that had taken place. Chad then took a roll of film to a one-hour developing service and explained to them that the photos showed an aborted baby. After doing some shopping, he returned to pick up the photos. He noticed that the employees were acting strangely when he paid for the photos and left.

That evening, after returning from a pro-life rally,

Chad noticed a police car parked at a convenience store near his home. He also noticed another police car at the end of his block. As Chad tells it, "A strange sense of fear shot through me, and I knew right away that something unpleasant was about to happen. We pulled into the driveway and suddenly the street in front of our house was FULL of police cars! There were at least eight cars there, plus a van from the coroner's office."

Police in battle fatigues, bullet-proof vests, and weapons approached Chad's house as though launching a drug bust. The detective in charge, John Hill, took Chad and his family inside the house for interrogation. He explained to Chad that employees at the photo shop had called the police department to report the mutilation and murder of a newborn baby. The employees apparently thought the child had been killed in a satanic ritual.

After Chad explained how he had found the baby and what had been done to it, the detective asked him if he would come down to police headquarters to make out a sworn statement. After two hours of interviews, Chad was released. No charges were filed against Chad by the police department, and the abortionist never came forward to file charges of burglary against Chad because of the potential for unwanted publicity and scrutiny of his practices.

Chad and other pro-lifers worked through December and into January 1990 to collect funds for a tombstone, a casket, and a gravesite for the aborted baby they named David. On 20 January 1990, just two days before the seventeenth anniversary of *Roe v. Wade*, Baby David was honored at a memorial service and buried with the respect that he never received at the hands of the abortionist.

The story does not end there, however. Chad and Debbie Hudnall, a pro-lifer from Houston, have reproduced photographs of Baby David on postcards and on large posters for pro-life pickets to use in showing the horrors of abortion in front of clinics. The postcards have been distributed by the thousands around the country to clearly show that abortion is the killing of an unborn child.

The Killing Continues

Every day in this country, an average of 4,320 Baby Davids die in abortion clinics. That means that every twenty seconds, one baby dies; every minute, three die; every hour, 180 die; every week, 30,240 die; every month, 129,600 die. Every year, 1,576,800 preborn or unborn children die at the hands of abortionists like Dr. George Tiller and those anonymous individuals who run the Women's Pavilion in Houston, Texas.

The radical feminists, Planned Parenthood spokesmen, and the abortionists themselves never want to discuss what actually happens during an abortion procedure; they prefer to discuss freedom of choice, personal autonomy, a woman's right to privacy, and other philosophical justifications as to why a woman should have the right to dispose of her unwanted fetus.

The advocates of child-killing, of course, seldom use the word baby to describe what is being killed. They prefer such euphemisms as fetus, product of conception, mass of tissue, and other terms which disguise the human life, the personhood, and the dignity of the child being killed in the womb.

The preborn baby, thanks to the U.S. Supreme Court, was dehumanized in *Roe v. Wade* and its companion decision, *Doe v. Bolton*, where the personhood of the child was discarded. As a non-person, the unborn child is without rights or protection from being killed by its mother and the abortionist.

There are a number of methods used to kill the baby, depending on the stage of development.

When the child is up to 12 weeks of age, the most common method is the use of a high-powered vacuum machine which sucks the baby out of the uterus. The vacuum is twenty-five times as powerful as the typical household vacuum cleaner. This technique is known as *suction curettage*. The suction is so powerful it literally tears the baby to pieces, limb by limb, until the baby is nothing more than shredded and torn body parts. Using this process, the baby's head is sometimes too large to fit through the suction tube. The doctor then inserts forceps into the uterus to crush the skull of the child so it can be sucked through the tube.

A second method of killing unborn babies is called D and E, or *dilatation and evacuation*. This procedure is performed when the baby is from four-to eight-months-old.

Using the D and E method, the doctor dilates the woman's cervix and places forceps into the uterus. He then starts grabbing whatever body parts are available and rips them out, piece by piece. The spine and skull are usually the last to be extracted. A curette or oval shaped knife is then used to scrape out whatever is left in the uterus.

A third method is D and C, or *dilatation and curettage*. This method uses a knife which is repeatedly rotated inside the womb to slice and hack the child into pieces. The body parts and placenta are then sucked out. The process of cutting a child to pieces is called *morcellation*.

A fourth method is the use of a saline solution, also known as *salting out the child*. This procedure is used between the fourth and seventh month. The abortionist withdraws a small amount of amniotic fluid and then replaces it with a salt solution. The baby swallows the salt and is poisoned; in addition, it is badly burned by the solution.

A fifth method is known as *hysterotomy*, performed in exactly the same way that a cesarean section is done. In this case, however, the object is to kill, not help the woman give birth to a baby.

A sixth method, which has fallen into disfavor, is the use of chemical *prostaglandins* which cause the woman to go into intense contractions which expel the baby from the womb. The baby usually dies during this process, but occasionally a mistake occurs, and the unwanted baby survives. It is then usually unattended and allowed to die. The possibility of having a live birth is the main reason this technique is seldom used today.

A seventh method is 100 percent effective. A poison, *digoxin*, is injected by needle directly into the baby's heart, killing it instantly. It is then removed by D and E or D and C.

An eighth method of killing late term unborn children has been developed by creative abortionists. The new process is called a *D and X*.

In this process, the abortionist turns the baby to a feet-first, face-down position within the womb. He then pulls the entire baby's body (except for the head) out of the uterus. Holding the baby's torso and kicking legs, the abortionist lifts the mother's cervix away from the baby's neck. He then jams a pair of scissors into the baby's skull. After opening the scissors to expand the wound, he inserts a suction catheter to suck out the baby's brains—ensuring the death of the child.

All of these techniques have been developed over time to ensure that the baby is effectively killed during the abortion process. Discussions centered on a woman's right to choose simply hide the fact that every time an abortion is performed, a baby boy or baby girl dies a violent death.

Planned Parenthood's Sordid Record

No discussion of the abortion industry would be complete without taking a brief look at Planned Parenthood and its history of support for abortion. It is also important to take a look at the life of Margaret Sanger, the founder of Planned Parenthood, who in the 1920s and 1930s, was well-known for her support of the pre-Nazi eugenics program designed to eliminate undesirable ethnic groups—ethnic cleansing.

Planned Parenthood is the largest abortion provider

in the U.S. and regularly receives at least $30 million a year in federal subsidies under the Public Health Services Act, Title X, program. Planned Parenthood not only supports abortion on demand as a constitutional right, but the organization has aggressively fought against adolescent parental consent or notification legislation and has opposed abortion clinic health and safety regulations. It has also fought against laws which mandate waiting periods for women seeking abortions.

Planned Parenthood also opposes laws which require informed consent of the mother before an abortion is performed. In 1978, for example, Planned Parenthood, the ACLU, and the National Abortion Rights Action League opposed an informed consent law passed by the city of Akron, Ohio.

The law did not prohibit abortion. What it did was require that a woman be informed of the biological development of her unborn child and of the potentially severe consequences of abortion, both physiological and psychological. Under this law, women were also required to be told of other options to abortion and provided with a list of agencies where they could get assistance if they decided not to abort.

The case eventually went to the U.S. Supreme Court. In 1983, the court, by a 5-4 decision, struck down Akron's ordinance, including the provisions that prohibited abortions on girls under fifteen without parental consent, as well as a twenty-four-hour waiting period for women after they had signed an informed consent form.

This is only one of numerous cases where Planned Parenthood has managed to defend the abortion industry from minimal standards.

Margaret Sanger's Legacy of Death

Planned Parenthood owes its existence and much of its pro-death philosophy to founder Margaret Sanger, a radical atheist and socialist.

Sanger formed the Voluntary Parenthood League in

1914, and in 1916 she opened up the first birth control clinic in the U.S. in Brooklyn, New York.

Sanger first married at eighteen, but quickly divorced and married William Sanger in 1902. She soon tired of fidelity to one man and began having numerous extramarital affairs. She even encouraged her husband to have affairs and once called marriage, "the most degenerating influence in the social order."[1] On another occasion, writing in her book, *Women and the New Race*, she observed that "The most merciful thing that the large family does to one of its infant members is to kill it."[2]

In order to promote her ideas on anarchy, socialism, free love and birth control, she founded a newspaper called *The Woman Rebel*. Its masthead bore the motto, "No gods, no masters."

In 1914 she travelled to England and met Dr. Havelock Ellis, a self-proclaimed sexologist who believed that all sexual conduct was normal. Ellis also believed that the poor should be sterilized and that euthanasia was a legitimate practice to eliminate useless individuals. Sanger had a short-lived affair with Ellis and then returned to the United States.

In the meantime, Sanger began investigating the occult in an attempt to communicate with her daughter who had died while she was in Europe with Ellis. This occult quest led her into contact with William Ralph Inge, dean of St. Paul's Cathedral in London.

Inge was a supporter of *eugenics*, the movement which taught that selective breeding could provide superior human beings. The Nazis, of course, also picked up on the eugenics philosophy and incorporated it into their extermination programs. Sanger eagerly adopted the idea of eugenics as a way of eliminating the so-called inferior races—which she felt to be all non-whites.

In her publication, *Birth Control Review*, November 1921, Sanger published an article which clearly reflected her racist philosophy: "Birth Control to Create a Race of Thoroughbreds." In the April 1932 issue of *Birth Control*

Review, she wrote that "the U.S. must apply a stern and rigid policy of sterilization and segregation to that grade of population whose progress is already tainted, or whose inheritance is such that objectionable traits may be transmitted to offspring."[3] In other writings, she referred to Jews, Blacks, and Hispanics as human weeds who needed to be eliminated.

Sanger was clearly sympathetic to the Nazis and their eugenics programs. In the April 1933 issue of *Birth Control Review*, Sanger published an article entitled "Eugenic Sterilization: An Urgent Need," by Dr. Ernest Rudin, Hitler's director of genetic sterilization and the founder of the Nazi Society for Racial Hygiene. Later that same year, Sanger published an article entitled "Selective Sterilization," by Leon Whitney, which praised Hitler's racial programs.

As Dr. George Grant has observed in *Grand Illusions: The Legacy of Planned Parenthood*,

> The bottom line is that Planned Parenthood was self-consciously organized, in part, to promote and enforce White Supremacy. Like the Ku Klux Klan, the Nazi Party, and the Mensheviks, it has been from its inception implicitly and explicitly racist. And this racist orientation is all too evident in its various programs and initiatives: birth control clinics, the abortion crusade, and sterilization initiatives.[4]

One would think that the leadership of Planned Parenthood would want to distance themselves from its founder, but just the opposite has happened in recent years. The past president of Planned Parenthood is Faye Wattleton, a woman who was honored by the American Humanist Association in 1986 as Humanist of the Year.

In accepting this honor, Wattleton told her audience, "I am truly honored to receive the Humanist of the Year Award. It means that I have one more thing in common with a woman who was a sister, nurse and the first leader of Planned Parenthood—Margaret Sanger, the founder of the family planning movement in this country and the recipient of the Humanist of the Year Award in 1957."[5]

In 1979, Wattleton celebrated Sanger's one hundredth birthday with these words, "As we celebrate the 100th birthday of Margaret Sanger, our outrageous and our courageous leader . . . we should be very proud of what we are and what our mission is. It is a very grand mission . . . abortion is only the tip of the iceberg."[6]

Planned Parenthood, the ACLU, the National Organization for Women, the National Abortion Rights Action League, and other pro-abortion groups are determined to keep baby killing legal in this country. They have been amazingly successful for twenty years. The Nazi death ethic is alive and well in the abortion rights movement.

The Legalization of Baby Killing

The year 1973 was significant for the unborn child. Two cases came before a very liberal Supreme Court that year which effectively legalized abortion on demand, for any reason, up to the point of the normal birth of the baby.

One case is well known: *Roe v. Wade*; the other is less well known, but it was just as destructive to the right to life: *Doe v. Bolton*.

The *Roe* decision declared that the unborn child had no personhood and therefore, no absolute right under the U.S. Constitution. The justices decided that the word *person* as used in the fourteenth amendment did not apply to the unborn fetus. They then arbitrarily divided a pregnancy into three trimesters. The court said that during the first three months of pregnancy, the state cannot enact any legislation protecting the baby; during the second trimester, the state can only pass laws which make the procedure safer for the mother; in the third trimester, the state can pass laws to protect the potential life of the child, but not if the health or life of the mother is in danger.

In the *Doe* case, the court defined the health of the mother to mean physical, emotional, psychological, familial, and complications which may arise as a result of the woman's age. If any of these factors would be threatened by prohibiting abortion, then they would overrule any concern one might have for the unborn baby.

In effect, these two decisions legalized abortion on demand at any stage of the unborn child's development.

Under these arbitrary rulings from the Supreme Court, the woman's right to autonomy and individual choice became primary. These cases upheld a woman's so-called right to privacy to kill her unborn child. It became simply a matter of her individual choice, regardless of the fact that her infant was being killed.

The court had effectively dehumanized the unborn child by stripping it of personhood and thus rendered it a nonperson. Again, we see Joseph Fletcher's concept of personhood impacting life and death decisions. Instead of viewing the unborn child as a human being and a person deserving of a right to life, these decisions simply redefined terms with euphemisms and left millions of babies to the hands of abortionists.

This prevailing ethic of autonomy supersedes the valid moral, personal, and cultural constraints upon the taking of a human life. By redefining someone as a nonperson, it is easy to justify compassionate killing for the sake of convenience or for economic reasons.

In recent Supreme Court decisions, the justices have made it a point to protect *Roe v. Wade* from being overturned, but they have made minor changes involving the public funding of abortion and tests for viability on unborn children.

The *Webster v. Reproductive Health Services* case, decided in 1989, upheld portions of a Missouri abortion law. The court rejected the trimester breakdown and allowed states to pass legislation regulating abortions back to the moment of conception. The court also rejected the argument that states were required to pay for abortions—although it maintained that a right to abortion still exists.

In the more recent *Planned Parenthood v. Casey* lawsuit, the U.S. Supreme Court ruled on a strict anti-abortion law passed in Pennsylvania. The court upheld portions of the law, including an informed consent clause which requires doctors and clinics to present women seeking abortions with information on abortion and fetal development. The court also upheld a mandatory twenty-four-hour waiting period as well as a requirement that women under eighteen obtain the consent of one parent or a judge before undergoing the operation.

The majority also ruled, however, that a woman seeking an abortion had no obligation to notify her husband of her intent to abort their child. The justices reasoned that this provision would endanger women who suffered from physical or psychological abuse at the hands of their spouses. "A state may not give to a man the kind of dominion over his wife that parents exercise over their children," said the court.

Although this decision was a slight victory for those concerned about the unborn, it contained some dangerous thinking that will ultimately lead to more abortions. In writing the majority decision, Justices Sandra Day O'Connor, Anthony M. Kennedy, and David Souter declared their support for the supposed constitutional right of a woman to kill her unborn child. They noted,

> Our obligation is to define the liberty of all, not to mandate our own moral code.... Our cases recognize the right of the individual, married or single, to be free from unwarranted governmental intrusion into matters so fundamentally affecting a person as the decision whether to bear or beget a child.... These matters, involving the most intimate and personal choices a person may make in a lifetime, choices central to personal dignity and autonomy, are central to the liberty protected by the Fourteenth Amendment. At the heart of liberty is the right to define one's own concept of existence, of meaning, of the universe, and of the mystery of human life....

What the court has done is elevate the right of a woman to kill her unborn child to a liberty guaranteed by the fourteenth amendment to the U.S. Constitution. As an ultimate example of personal autonomy, the wife has no obligation to inform her husband of the decision to kill *their* child.

This moves the concept of abortion rights beyond simply a right to privacy to a liberty right which is nearly absolute. In my opinion this decision, as well as the original decisions legalizing abortion on demand, are nothing more than examples of radical social engineering by a few unelected individuals who have decided to abrogate the right to life of the unborn.

In dehumanizing the child to the status of a nonperson, and by elevating personal autonomy to an absolute right, the U.S. Supreme Court is dooming millions of unborn children to death.

As a physician, and one who has studied fetal development, it is absolutely unconscionable that a modern court could still maintain the fiction that the unborn baby is not a person, but a potential life. With our current medical knowledge, it is an unmistakable scientific and biological fact that human life begins at the moment of conception. It is not a potential life, but an actual life that should be accorded the protection of our laws.

Tragically, our U.S. Supreme Court justices cannot seem to grasp, or choose to ignore, these simple concepts and continue to philosophize about choice, autonomy, and liberty for the woman, while ignoring the unborn children who are being killed for convenience in abortion clinics across our land.

Chapter 6

Killing Handicapped Newborns

The mid-1970s was an exciting time for the field of pediatric surgery and pediatric care of critically ill newborns. During this period, new technologies were developed which enabled us to save the lives of children who would have died had they been born in earlier years. These new life-saving techniques, though, also brought ethical dilemmas along with them. Physicians were suddenly faced with new questions in dealing with ill or handicapped newborns. Should physicians treat severely handicapped newborns who had no chance of living productive lives? Should a doctor save the life of a retarded child who will place emotional and financial burdens on his family for years to come? These and other ethical questions faced us as we adjusted to the new technologies.

As a pro-life pediatrician, I began to take an active interest in bioethical issues involving fetal harvesting, treatment of handicapped children, and related ethical dilemmas. My interest in these issues led me eventually to become a founding member of the American Academy of Pediatrics Committee on Bioethics in 1981.

Those inside and outside of our profession who held to a quality of life ethic, instead of a sanctity of life ethic, were eager to make their opinions known. To them, the quick fix was to just let these unwanted children die of neglect—or to actively kill them. The compassionate killers were on the move to normalize infanticide as acceptable medical practice.

The pro-death enthusiasts were bold in their pronouncements. For example, in May 1973, James Watson, a Nobel Laureate and discoverer of the DNA double helix, made the following statement:

> If a child were not declared alive until three days after birth, then all parents could be allowed the choice only a few are given under the present system. The doctor could allow the child to die if the parents so choose and save a lot of misery and suffering. I believe this view is the only rational, compassionate attitude to have.[1]

And in January, 1978, Nobel Laureate Francis Crick told the Pacific News Service: "No newborn infant should be declared human until it has passed certain tests regarding its genetic endowment and that if it fails these tests, it forfeits the right to live."[2]

It was Dr. Joseph Fletcher, of course, who designed the continuum which placed the unborn child in the category of a nonperson and who placed the senile individual in the same distinction. Under Fletcher's continuum, only the fully rational adult was to be granted personhood. Using his arbitrary definition of personhood, all others in various stages of development were only considered potential persons.

In 1973, Fletcher wrote the following in the *American Journal of Nursing*:

> It is ridiculous to give ethical approval to the positive ending of subhuman life in utero, as we do now in therapeutic abortions for reasons of mercy and compassion, but refuse to approve of positively ending a subhuman life in extremis. If we are morally obliged to put an end to a pregnancy when an amniocentesis reveals a terribly defective fetus, we are equally obliged

to put an end to a patient's hopeless misery when a brain scan reveals that a patient with cancer has advanced brain mestastes.[3]

Fletcher describes abortion as an act of mercy and compassion and then tells his readers that if we can justify abortion, we are morally obliged to justify the killing of handicapped newborns.

As more and more bioethicists began lobbying for infanticide, their thinking began to impact the medical field—especially among pediatricians and pediatric surgeons. The results of a survey of these physicians, published in *Pediatrics*, in October 1977, showed the dangerous shift that had taken place in the minds of these doctors.

The survey asked a number of questions dealing with the ethics of withholding or withdrawing treatment from handicapped newborns. Question One asked: "Do you believe that the life of each and every newborn infant should be saved if it is within our ability to do so?"

The results of this survey were shocking to me. Of the pediatric surgeons who were asked this question, 83 percent said no—they didn't feel they had an obligation to save each infant in their care. Of the pediatricians questioned, 81 percent said no.[4]

With such attitudes being adopted by physicians and being reinforced by self-proclaimed bioethicists and scientists, the rush toward legalizing infanticide probably would have been accomplished by the mid-1980s. Fortunately, an event occurred in 1982 that caused a firestorm of controversy and dealt the compassionate killers a devastating blow.

The Baby Doe Case

On 9 April 1982, a Downs syndrome baby was born in Bloomington, Indiana. The baby was not only retarded, but had an obstruction in the esophagus that prevented normal eating. The tracheo-esophageal fistula was easily treated, but both the parents and the physician agreed to allow the baby to die by starvation. In order to facilitate the starvation process, the parents and physician went to court and received the court's blessing to allow the child to die. On 15 April the baby died of starvation—but Baby Doe's death did not go unnoticed by then-Surgeon General C. Everett Koop and the pro-life Reagan administration.

Baby Doe's death by starvation hit the nation's newspapers and shocked the country into the realization that something terribly wrong had occurred.

In response to Doe's death, President Reagan worked with the U.S. attorney general and the secretary of the Department of Health and Human Services to investigate the starvation of Doe as discrimination against a handicapped person. In May, HHS issued a "Notice to Health Care Providers" who received federal funding. The notice stated that under section 504 of the Rehabilitation Act of 1973, it was unlawful for a physician to withhold nutritional sustenance or necessary medical care from handicapped infants.

The controversy over Baby Doe raged on for over two years as physicians, hospital administrators, and the federal government debated ways of handling future cases involving handicapped newborns.

In March of 1983, the Department of Health and Human Services issued a rule which required that health care facilities receiving federal aid post a notice in hospitals saying: "Discriminatory failure to feed and care for handicapped infants in this facility is prohibited by federal law." The notice included a twenty-four-hour toll free number people could use to report suspicious hospital behavior in dealing with handicapped children.

On 14 April 1983, Judge Gerhard Gesell struck down the Baby Doe rule as a result of a lawsuit filed by the American Academy of Pediatrics (AAP), the National Association of Children's Hospitals and Related Institutions, and the Children's Hospital National Medical Center in Washington, D.C. These organizations sued to have the

Baby Doe orders abolished because they felt the federal government was being too intrusive in the medical profession. In an attempt to reach a compromise solution, the academy offered a proposal which would require hospitals to establish infant bioethical review committees as a condition to receiving federal funds.

In July of 1984, the AAP and nineteen other organizations reached an agreement with six U.S. senators on legislation concerning the treatment of severely disabled newborns. The legislation eventually ended up as part of a law dealing with child abuse.

As a founding member of the AAP's committee on bioethics, I was involved in developing the policies and statements that eventually led to the passage of this law prohibiting discrimination against handicapped newborns. In the policy statement of the AAP, which was issued in August 1983, the following was stated:

> The major difficulty for the pediatrician is in knowing the interests of the patient. The attending physician may not have access to all the relevant facts, including the proper diagnosis, prognosis, or alternatives for treatment. His/her judgment may be distorted by pressures from patients or others, as well as by personal biases and feelings. The complexity and importance of these decisions require that they be made with the utmost care. The traditional method of a single physician making such judgments, experience, and points of view, may lead to decisions which, in retrospect, cannot be justified.
>
> To ensure that such profound judgments are made in as careful and informed a manner as can reasonably be achieved, we believe such decisions should be made only after thorough review. Ideally, such review should include consultation with individuals and medical, legal, ethical and social expertise. Individuals with the desired expertise will not be available in all settings, and not all cases allow time for the datagathering and reflection that is desirable. In the vast majority of such cases, however, time and personnel

are available to allow for a more thorough analysis of the decision than can be achieved by a single physician, with or without the involvement of parents.

In addition to promoting patient interests, consultation will protect physicians from charges of hasty or negligent decisions. To serve the interests of patients and physicians, however, there must be accountability, in the form of an institutionally-approved group such as an ethics consultation committee. How such groups are formed, what procedures they should follow, and other procedural issues need to be worked out. Extensive experience with institutional review boards for the review of ethical problems involving research on human subjects suggests that such groups can be effective and constructive.[5]

In working with the Department of Health and Human Services, the American Academy of Pediatrics and other medical societies gained support for the idea of establishing these bioethics committees in hospitals where neonatal intensive care units were operating. On 29 November 1983, these medical groups issued the "Principles of Treatment of Disabled Infants," which ended up as part of the HHS rules and regulations published in the *Federal Register*. The principles stated were as follows:

When medical care is clearly beneficial, it should always be provided. . . .

Considerations such as anticipated or actual limited potential of an individual and present or future lack of available community resources are irrelevant and must not determine the decisions concerning medical care. The individual's medical condition should be the sole focus of the decision. These are very strict standards.

It is ethically and legally justified to withhold medical or surgical procedures which are clearly futile and will only prolong the act of dying. However, supportive care should be provided, including sustenance as medically indicated and relief of pain and suffering.

The needs of the dying person should be respected. The family also should be supported in its grieving.

In cases where it is uncertain whether medical treatment will be beneficial, a person's disability must not be the basis for a decision to withhold treatment. . . . When doubt exists at any time about whether to treat, a presumption always should be in the favor of treatment.[6]

My Growing Concern Over Ethical Dilemmas

As I watched the Baby Doe case unfold in the papers and in the professional literature, I realized that significant decisions were going to be made in how the pediatric profession dealt with future Baby Doe cases. I decided that I wanted to become part of the policy-making process within the American Academy of Pediatrics and asked to become a founding member of the newly formed Committee on Bioethics. This committee was formed primarily as a defensive measure to head off any further federal controls over the practice of medicine.

My primary motivation for joining the bioethics committee was to make sure that the pro-life position was given some consideration in any policy decisions being made. I was also concerned about ethical issues because of my position as director of the critical care unit at Sacred Heart Children's Hospital in Pensacola. I was involved in training residents, worked with physicians in neonatal intensive care units, and dealt day to day with clinical problems involving handicapped newborns. I was also very interested in the direction that organ transplantation was taking—especially as it involved the dilemma of fetal harvesting. In my role, it was imperative that I be involved in developing compassionate policies in dealing with chronically ill and handicapped children.

My interest in saving the lives of handicapped children went back to 1969 when I joined the staff of Sacred Heart Hospital in Pensacola. As I followed the medical literature on new technologies in treating the handicapped, it occurred to me that we could probably develop some of these techniques to help save lives.

In 1973, the hospital employed its first pediatrician, Dr. Edward Westmark, devoted to newborn care. He trained himself to provide competent care to the at risk newborns. At that time, very few neonatology units were operating in this country. In response, Dr. Westmark set up a training program to train nurses and doctors in the management of sick or handicapped newborns.

We set up the neonatal intensive care unit and then developed an extensive transportation system to bring in ill newborns from outlying areas. My mother donated $5,000 to the hospital to renovate a van as a neonatal intensive care unit on wheels. The van was equipped with an incubator and other equipment needed to sustain a critically ill newborn being transported to the neonatal intensive care unit (NICU).

Later we were allowed the use of a Navy helicopter and eventually a fixed wing aircraft to transport newborns and children who needed care. In time, our hospital became the regional care unit for pregnant mothers who were at risk, as well as for critically ill neonates. Eventually, an entire network of regional neonatal intensive care units (RHICUs) was developed throughout the state of Florida with fine working relationships with the University Schools of Medicine, notably the University of Florida School of Medicine in Gainesville.

In addition, the Florida Pediatric Society employed a professional lobbyist in the capital, Tallahassee, and successfully established a state Department of Children's Medical Services.

My interest in bioethics evolved from these activities as I worked and taught at Sacred Heart.

Establishing Bioethics Guidelines

The bioethics committee's first task was to take a long and hard look at the facts surrounding the starvation of Baby Doe and their significance to the field of pediatrics.

We debated vigorously as to the appropriate response to this ethical dilemma. Dr. Eugene Diamond, a Catholic, and myself, a conservative Protestant, were the only two members of the committee who held to a pro-life viewpoint. The rest of the members of the committee were libertarians, most of whom were actively involved in the American Civil Liberties Union.

Surprisingly enough, however, our committee eventually found common agreement and issued guidelines in developing infant care bioethics committees in hospitals with neonatal intensive care units. In our final report, which was published in *Pediatrics*, August 1984, we wrote:

> Although the precise membership of the committee will depend on institutional needs and resources, it is important that the committee include members from various disciplines. A multidisciplinary approach is recommended so that the committee will have sufficient expertise to supply and evaluate all pertinent information, and because representation of viewpoints of the community is desirable to contribute to better decisions.
>
> An effort should be made to ensure that the committee has at least the following expertise available to it through members or advisors: medical, psychosocial, human service resources, nursing, social work, and familiarity with issues affecting disabled persons, legal and ethical. The committee may wish to identify and have available other areas of expertise.
>
> The committee size should be large enough to represent diversity, but not so large as to hinder candid discussions and deliberations. The following is a suggested list of core committee members: practicing physician; pediatrician knowledgeable about the nursery; nurse; hospital administrator; parent of a disabled child; representative of a disability group, or developmental disability expert; social worker; member of the hospital's pastoral program or other clergy; lawyer; lay community member; and person trained in ethics or philosophy.[9]

Our recommendation that each hospital with a neonatal unit establish a bioethics committee proved to be very successful in stopping the development of infanticide as acceptable medical practice.

The committees are only advisory in nature yet performed a much-needed service by providing physicians and parents with an alternative viewpoint in dealing with serious medical ethical dilemmas. There remained, however, the possibility of resorting to the courts in the event that strong disagreements occurred over the recommendations given.

On-the-Job Training

I became the chairman of the bioethics committee at Sacred Heart and can attest to the importance of such committees in dealing with the treatment of ill and handicapped newborns and children. In my experience, only once did consideration of a resort to the court develop, and this case was eventually dropped.

Our committee met routinely nearly every week for a year-and-a-half as we wrestled with a variety of ethical dilemmas. As consultative services were provided to the physicians and parents, we were able to convert our recommendations into appropriate policies and procedures which would apply to future cases. Eventually, the bioethics committee's work in providing review and advice diminished as the hospital's infant care protocols were developed. We met less frequently, dealing only with extraordinary cases not covered by the precedent of past ethical dilemmas.

We reached decisions overwhelmingly unanimously after much discussion of the case at hand. A confidential advisory report was issued which included any dissent. The report was discussed with the physician and the parent where agreement proved to be universal. What amazed me was how well this deliberative system worked to assure satisfactory agreement in the management of the patients and avoiding infanticide.

I did not realize it at the time, but the American Academy of Pediatrics and its bioethics committee recommendation successfully stopped the acceptance of infanticide in the medical profession. I believe we have that same opportunity in halting acceptance of euthanasia of the elderly, the chronically ill, and the handicapped. Unfortunately, we are very close to losing this euthanasia battle unless there is a concerted effort among physicians to speak against the Derek Humphrys and the Jack Kevorkians. We again need aggressive support of public professional and advocacy groups in opposing the euthanasia movement.

I believe there remains the need to sustain the role and concept of institutional bioethics committees in dealing with medical ethical dilemmas to assure true compassionate care while avoiding killing. It is vital that we err on the side of life in the medical ethical decision-making process.

The Academy's Schizophrenia

The American Academy of Pediatrics performed a tremendous service in halting infanticide, but my experience with the academy has not always been positive.

There is a strong libertarian mentality that is deeply entrenched within the academy bureaucracy and its various functions. The academy, for example, remains adamant in its support for abortion on demand—even though abortion constitutes prenatal infanticide.

In previous years, attempts to pass a number of resolutions out of the bioethics committee condemning and opposing such things as condoned suicide, pedophilia, incest, and homosexuality have failed. Attempts to pass a resolution expressing support for the two-parent family also failed in early forums and committee activities.

Why is the academy so reluctant to publicly oppose condoned suicide, child molestation, and homosexuality? Or to support the two-parent family? The answer lies in the philosophy and the ethic of radical autonomy which has captured the minds of many of the physicians who are on the committees. I can recall one member of our bioethics committee actually revealing that he thought that adult/child sex could actually be beneficial to the child. This is a noted pediatrician who worked on the committees creating policies supposedly designed to benefit children. Would this be compatible with the academy's strong support of child abuse laws, including sexual abuse? Part of his problem is the concept of children's rights, including freedom of sexual expression as long as it is not harmful or coerced—children's autonomy rights!

While we achieved unusual success in stopping infanticide, there are still those in the medical community who think that handicapped or chronically ill children are less than human and are obligated to forfeit their God-given right to life. I am convinced that although we managed to halt the neglect or killing of newborns as accepted medical practice, there will continue to be an aggressive minority who will push for the killing of those children who are viewed as defective.

Under the Clinton administration, we can assume this pro-death movement will gain renewed vigor—especially in the area of fetal harvesting. In his third day in office, President Clinton signed an executive order overturning the Reagan-Bush ban on fetal research. This will undoubtedly open up a flood of medical research and will give abortionists a market for the babies they routinely kill.

Fetal Harvesting and the Devaluing of Human Life

As I mentioned earlier, one of my primary concerns in the mid-seventies and eighties was how the medical profession was going to handle the issue of *fetal harvesting*. There is now a renewed push to use fetal brain cells as a treatment for Parkinson's victims, and if not stopped, this utilitarian concept could develop into a major growth industry for the abortionists.

As Dr. Curt Harris, an endocrinologist and bioethicist, noted in an article in *Physician* magazine several years ago, the harvesting of organs from aborted babies is unethical for a number of reasons:

1. Authentic consent from the patient is impossible. He notes that under a code of ethics developed after the Nazi Nuremberg Trials, "... no human can be the subject of experimental research without his or her full knowledge and consent."

2. The use of fetal tissue in research will serve as an inducement to abortion. The woman who is confused about whether or not to abort her child will see some good coming out of her decision to abort. She will be more inclined to kill her child than she might have been. The abortionist will also see the financial possibilities in urging women to abort their children. According to Harris, the fetal tissue industry is a potential $6 billion-a-year business. As Harris notes,

> There is no question that the fresh collection of tissue would require close cooperation between the abortionist and the researcher performing transplantation. Timing, sex selection, and even choice of the procedure would become routine criteria in abortions if we begin harvesting our unborn.

3. Accepting fetal tissue obtained from induced abortion means becoming an accomplice to the crime after the fact. The Nazi psychiatrist who collected Jewish brains and skeletons was considered just as guilty as the SS troops who provided the body parts. The physician who rationalizes the killing of babies to use as spare parts is just as guilty as the abortionist and the mother who consents to the killing. We cannot allow fetal tissue researchers to encourage the abortionists to create a new medical service in baby brain cells.[8]

The Loma Linda Experiment

Up until 1988, Loma Linda University Medical Center in California was conducting experiments on harvesting organs from *anencephalic infants*. These are infants born without cortical brain functions (the area of the brain which controls consciousness) but still maintain brain stem function (that part of the brain which controls autonomic reactions such as breathing and heart pumping).

In Loma Linda, however, there was an effort to redefine when brain death occurred so that fresh organs could be harvested from living children. When the pro-life community learned of these experiments at Loma Linda, it caused such an uproar that the medical center stopped doing transplantation experiments on these infants.

In December of 1987, Loma Linda had established a policy to deal with anencephalic children. The policy stated that these infants would receive ventilator (breathing) support at birth and then be monitored for up to seven days or until all brain functions had ceased. The hope was that these infants would die quickly so their organs could be used, but most failed to meet brain death criteria within the period hoped for.

Redefining Death to Include Living Babies

In an effort to get the best use out of anencephalic baby organs, legislators and medical personnel attempted to have the definition of brain death changed to include live anencephalic infants. They were to be considered dead under a newly created category called "respiratory brain death".

By attempting to expand the definition of brain death (which is defined as the death of cortical and brain stem functions), the researchers were unwittingly opening up a whole new controversy: that of harvesting the organs from living, but unconscious or retarded humans.

If these researchers had succeeded in expanding the definition of death to include living anencephalic infants, the compassionate killers would have had additional reasons to justify the harvesting of organs from retarded adults or those in a persistent vegetative state. After all, they would reason, why not get some good use out of these body parts? Why watch a mentally ill patient vegetate in a mental institution, when his organs could be used to benefit others? The Nazi doctors gave these same reasons as they justified their experiments on living persons in the concentration camps. After all, if the person is going to be killed anyway, why not contribute to the advancement of science by experimenting on them?

This new definition of brain death, if adopted, would have thrilled those like pro-death bioethicist Peter Singer who once said,

> If we compare a severely defective human infant with a nonhuman animal, a dog or a pig, for example, we will often find the nonhuman to have superior capacities, both actual and potential, for rationality, self-consciousness, communication, and anything else that can plausibly be considered morally significant. Only the fact that the defective infant is a member of the species, *Homo Sapiens*, leads it to be treated differently from the dog or pig. Species membership alone, however, is not morally relevant.[9]

The point Peter Singer misses is that the species *homo sapiens* is distinctly different than any species of the animal world because we are created in the image of God; we have a value that is higher than that of animals in God's world. We have an inherent right to life that is God-given. It is a sacred right that must be respected, regardless of how defective we might be.

The anencephalic infant does not cease to be human because it is severely handicapped and has only a few days to live. Under no circumstances should these infants have their organs harvested while they are still alive.

The pro-death philosophers, though, could easily justify taking organs from living humans by simply changing the definition of when death occurs—or, by denying that anencephalics are persons under Joseph Fletcher's narrow definition of personhood. His definition of personhood would include the mentally retarded, thus opening them up for potential harvesting.

Justified Organ Transplantation

In my view, there should be no more research done on the use of fetal tissues in aiding Parkinson's victims or in treating other disorders. There is a line which physicians and researchers should not cross. That line is that a living handicapped infant or a retarded individual is not to be declared a non-person and their body parts used to benefit someone else. This constitutes unethical medical practice and should be unlawful. There are other valid alternatives to help Parkinson's victims. One of those alternatives is the use of tissue cultures grown in a laboratory. This is a promising area of research and one that could benefit Parkinson's victims without encouraging more abortions.

But what of organ transplants in general? I do not oppose the harvesting of organs from children or adults who are declared clinically and legally dead. The harvesting of organs is a complicated process, requiring a number of legal safeguards, but for the most part our profession has been ethical in its approach to organ transplantation.

At Sacred Heart Hospital, for example, we often faced situations where a child was the victim of a drowning. After being declared legally dead using the brain death criteria, we would keep the child on a ventilator and circulatory support as a candidate for organ harvesting. This procedure was done only with parental informed consent when there was a suitable recipient of the organs. A medical team would fly in from the city where the recipient was waiting, perform the operation in our hospital and fly back to their hospital to transplant the organ or organs.

This is a valid and ethical procedure to benefit someone else. The point is that if the patient is dead, there is no moral prohibition against taking his organs, as long as permission is granted from parents or guardians.

The harvesting of organs from not yet dead infants, however, is immoral and should never be permitted. We should resist any efforts to redefine brain death or to redefine the comatose or retarded person as a nonhuman in order to take his organs. This, quite simply, would be killing.

Chapter 7

Killing as Medical Treatment

As I write this chapter, Dr. Jack Kevorkian, nicknamed Dr. Death in the media, has been embroiled in a controversy stemming from complications resulting from his thirteenth assisted suicide in Michigan. (As of this time, Kevorkian has assisted in the deaths of fifteen persons.)

According to news reports, a right-to-life activist found a document in a Kevorkian associate's garbage which detailed the assisted killing of seventy-year-old Hugh Gale. According to this document, Gale panicked after Kevorkian's carbon monoxide gas mask was placed over his face. The first time Gale cried, "Take it off," the mask was removed. The second time he panicked, however, the mask stayed on, and he died.

Prosecutor Richard Thompson told reporters that "this document . . . with him asking the mask be taken off and the mask was continued, takes it out of the realm of assisted suicide and puts it into the realm of attempted homicide." Regrettably, however, no murder charges were filed against Kevorkian.

Investigators also apparently found another document on Gale's death in Kevorkian's apartment. This document showed signs of being altered to hide the fact that Gale had screamed a second time to have the mask removed. Thompson had tried to prosecute Kevorkian for his first three assisted suicides, but the cases were dismissed. At that time, Michigan had no law prohibiting assisted suicides.

When interviewed by reporters, Kevorkian's attorney, Geoffrey Fieger said, "A bunch of right-wing Christian nuts again called Dr. Kevorkian a murderer. It's laughable."

In an emergency legislative vote, the Michigan House and Senate voted in late February 1993 to approve a law that makes assisted suicide a crime punishable by up to four years in prison and a $2,000 fine. This law is to remain in effect for twenty-one months while the issue is studied by a commission. Kevorkian has been busy helping people kill themselves since the Michigan legislature indicated it would ban his activities.

His tenth victim was eighty-two-year-old Stanley Ball; his eleventh was seventy-three-year-old Mary Biernat. Both died of carbon monoxide poisoning in Ball's home in Michigan. Biernat's children had driven her from Indiana to Michigan to be assisted in dying by Kevorkian.

Only weeks earlier, Kevorkian helped another man kill himself. The ninth victim of Kevorkian's medicide was Jack Elmer Miller, fifty-three. Miller inhaled carbon monoxide through a mask in his home in Wayne's County, Huron Township in Michigan. Miller had been diagnosed with bone cancer in June of 1992 and was told in January 1993 that he had just a few weeks to live. Miller's five children and fiancee, Cynthia Lee Coffey, were apparently present when he killed himself.

According to news reports, Coffey initially contacted Kevorkian and described Miller's desire to kill himself. Kevorkian, of course, was more than willing to oblige. After the killing, Kevorkian's attorney Geoffrey Fieger told reporters, "There will be more deaths. There is a feeling of desperation among many people out there that time is running out."[1]

At the time of Miller's death, the prosecutor who was investigating the case told reporters he wasn't certain if

Kevorkian would be charged. "If you have a direct, intense action that causes the death, then that's a homicide. If you don't have direct involvement, then that's what's being referred to as assisted suicide. That's a gray, murky area right now."

As the Michigan legislature was debating passing a law to prohibit physician-assisted suicide, Kevorkian was telling reporters, "Euthanasia and abortion and assisted suicide are medical issues that are legitimate procedures. They've become controversial because religion has meddled in it." He also told news sources what he will do if the law is passed, "They [the legislature] can pass any law they want against physician-assisted suicide, and I'll break it immediately."[2]

Dr. Jack Kevorkian's brand of medicine is not new. The Nazis practiced it with great enthusiasm, and the Dutch are currently practicing "compassionate" killing.

Kevorkian is a retired pathologist who has had a long and morbid interest in death and in the harvesting of body organs. At one point in his career, he decided that it would be a waste of organs to simply execute condemned murderers and bury them. He suggested that, in the interest of science, these murderers be subjected to experimental drugs and controversial surgical procedures to help others. He also recommended that prisoners' brains would provide scientists with a unique opportunity to study an intact, *living* brain.

In addition, he felt it would be wasteful to not use every available body part to help others. He proposed an auction market where rich people would bid for these organs and the money earned from the auction could be used to provide the poor with free organs. You may recall the German university professor who collected Jewish skulls and skeletons and the physicians in the death camps who sought to benefit science by experimenting on live subjects. The parallel between what the Nazi doctors did in the camps and what Kevorkian is either doing or recommending is unmistakable.

In 1988, Kevorkian contacted Hemlock Society founder Derek Humphry and asked him to join forces to establish a suicide clinic which would provide the Kevorkian brand of "Medicide": planned death. Humphry refused, telling Kevorkian that he's a law reformer not a law breaker. Yet, as we will see, Humphry's stand on compassionate killing is really not much different than Kevorkian's.

Kevorkian's first killing occurred in June of 1990. He helped Janet Adkins, an Alzheimer's sufferer to kill herself and on the following day he gave an interview to the *New York Times* about his action.

Adkins had recently joined the Hemlock Society and was a member of the Unitarian Church. She had approached three doctors in Oregon asking them to kill her, but none would oblige. She learned of Kevorkian's service in 1989 and saw his death machine explained in detail on Phil Donahue's talk program.

After contacting Kevorkian, Adkins flew to Royal Oak, Michigan, with her husband and ended up killing herself with Kevorkian's help in a 1968 Volkswagen van at a campsite in Oakland County, Michigan. Although Kevorkian was charged with murder, the case was dropped because of the lack of a law prohibiting assisted suicide.

I would have to agree with the view of Professor George Annas of Boston University school of medicine who noted that Kevorkian is more like a serial killer than a physician.[3]

Is Something Wrong With This Picture?

Dr. Kevorkian's mission in life is to practice medicide, (the killing of patients), instead of providing for patients' healing or comfort. He is the modern day equivalent of the Nazi doctors who killed to relieve individuals of the burden of their lives. He is proud of his work in killing. According to Derek Humphry, writing in *Final Exit*, Kevorkian's business card reads: "Jack Kevorkian, M.D., Bioethics and Obiatry. Special death counseling."

Kevorkian defines obiatry as "going to your death with the aid of your physician."

Kevorkian and other proponents of so-called "death with dignity" are pushing for the acceptance of compassionate killing as a legitimate part of medical practice. In fact, if their goal comes to fruition, it is likely that this service will eventually be covered under insurance plans and funded by the government and an entire new industry will develop to complement the abortion clinics dispensing death to unborn children.

It might even occur to the abortionists to capitalize on this new killing business by expanding abortion clinics to include a number of other services, including killing depressed teen-agers, chronically ill adults, and the handicapped—all paid for by insurance companies or the government. This may sound far-fetched, but Kevorkian has already suggested setting up suicide clinics for the purpose of assisting in providing efficient and effective means of killing oneself.

Derek Humphry's Death Wish

In August of 1991, Derek Humphry's book, *Final Exit*, became a best-seller in the U.S. The book is a philosophical justification for condoned suicide and physician-assisted suicide. The term *self-deliverance* is used to describe killing oneself. After describing some of the more messy ways of killing oneself through shooting, drowning, hangings, electrocution, car exhausts, etc., Humphry provides the reader with a recipe list of poisons to use in committing suicide. He also recommends putting a plastic bag around your head and securing it with a rubber band, just to make certain you eventually stop breathing.

It is not known exactly how many people have killed themselves as a result of using his book, but the last figure I gleaned from news reports indicates that Humphry's instructions have resulted in more deaths than Kevorkian's death machine.

Humphry is noted for having helped kill his first wife,

Jean, who had been diagnosed with cancer. He gave her a lethal injection and kept two pillows handy to smother her in case the poison failed to take. He deserted his second wife, Ann, after discovering she had cancer. He also apparently encouraged her to kill herself, and eventually she obliged. Although he is no longer head of the Hemlock Society, Humphry's influence is still felt through his writings.

The Hemlock Society has been active in getting pro-death initiatives placed on the ballot recently in both California and Washington state. Both were narrowly defeated. (More on this later.)

The Humphrys and Kevorkians will continue to push their death agenda in state legislatures, in the media, in academia; and now, with the predominate materialist, utilitarian secular philosophy and its ethic of radical autonomy, they will most likely have little difficulty gaining policy changes within federal and state legislatures to legitimize compassionate killing as a medical service.

What is the Death Agenda and Why Should We Oppose It?

In Greek, the word *euthanasia* means "good or happy death." What it means in the strictest of terms is the taking of the life of another individual, either by encouraging them to die or by assisting them in dying.

The killing can be accomplished by withholding or withdrawing treatment and/or sustenance, or by committing an act that will kill the patient. Thus, euthanasia is commonly termed either active or passive. Voluntary euthanasia denotes a patient choosing to be allowed to die or to be aided in dying. Non-voluntary euthanasia denotes that the patient is incompetent and cannot provide informed consent or make a decision for himself. Here the decision to allow to die or to aid in dying is made by another individual, called a substituted judgment. Another individual's judgment is substituted for the patient's. This may be the nearest of kin, a designated (living will or durable power of attorney) individual or the court appointment of a guardian.

Another category of euthanasia is termed involuntary euthanasia, the killing of someone without their consent and/or knowledge—better known as homicide.

Killing or Caring?

The killing of patients as compassionate medical care is proposed as a solution to end suffering, pain, and a burdensome life considered no longer worthy to be lived. But, as we will see, these are invalid justifications for killing the handicapped, the chronically ill, the senile, or the simply unwanted individual.

In traditional medicine, the duty of the doctor is to do everything he can to heal the patient; failing that, it is his duty to relieve suffering and to make the patient as comfortable as possible in the natural process of dying—comfort care. If death is eminent, the doctor is obligated to allow the patient to die naturally of the disease. This is ethical medical practice. The doctor is also under no obligation to prolong dying by futile treatment. It is his duty, however, to never participate in knowingly and intentionally hastening death by killing.

With our increased technological abilities, one of the great fears facing patients today is that they will be kept alive artificially for years on machines or through other life-sustaining measures. Some of these measures are termed extraordinary, such as ventilators, cardiac assistance, blood pressure sustenance, etc., which will keep the patient alive even after the person has experienced brain death.

No one recommends keeping a person on artificial life support after they are legally considered dead by standards of (1) irreversible cessation of cardio-respiratory function, or (2) brain death, the irreversible cessation of cerebral cortical and brain stem function. The only temporary exception is the harvesting of tissue and/or organs for transplantation. The decision to withhold or withdraw life-sustaining measures is exercised by the patient (in consultation with the doctor), if competent to make such a decision. If incompetent, then a substituted judgment is made on the patient's behalf by a prior self-determination—the living will or by someone who is designated to make those decisions for him, a durable power of attorney, or rarely the court.

Unfortunately, the technological advances we have made in prolonging vital functions add to the high cost of medical care, and this has been used by pro-death doctors to justify allowing-to-die (passive euthanasia) and consideration of aid-in-dying (active euthanasia) for patients whose prognosis for recovery seems to be slim. A third element complicates this process: third party payers, i.e, government insurance (Medicaid, Medicare), private health insurers, and hospital administration, who are held accountable for controlling health care costs. Significant financial risks are at stake and the physician responsible for the patient's health services may be tacitly, it not explicitly, obligated to limit access to uncompensated care. Pressure mounts steadily to ration health care and, in fact, is occurring de facto. Thus, third parties through restrictive reimbursement policy may and commonly do impede physicians and administrators of health care facilities from making judgments based on the primary best interest of the patient because of cost factors.

Err on the Side of Life

In working with a terminally ill patient, it is the doctor's duty to alleviate pain as much as possible. This is most often accomplished through narcotics and/or regional anesthesia. In an effort to stop pain, narcotics may impede and compromise cardio-respiratory function and actually hasten death. It is a difficult but manageable challenge to find the balance between effective pain control for the patient without compromising recovery or even hastening death.

The basic premise upon which the traditional doctor

practices ethical medicine is to err on the side of life. We are not called upon to prolong the natural dying process, but we are to provide pain control and comfort care including the provision of sustenance—food and liquids.

The care and treatment of patients in an irreversible coma or the ill-defined persistent vegetative state (PVS) are most problematic. These are individuals who may be ventilator-dependent or require life-sustaining cardio-vascular support to sustain vital organ functions. The cortical brain function is absent or severely impaired. These individuals do not meet brain death criteria yet are severely neurologically impaired or comatose. Though alive, they have not ceased to be human beings and warrant our care and respect as incapacitated, disabled persons.

There are now an estimated ten thousand individuals in the U.S. who are in a persistent vegetative state. The federal Patient Self-Determination Act of 1990 has been implemented by the states, requiring all patients entering health care facilities that receive Medicaid and Medicare funding (essentially all) to execute a living will, or its equivalent, defining the patient's wishes in case of incapacitation—irreversible coma or PVS. This specifically relates to the withholding or withdrawal of life-sustaining measures, including sustenance.

In unprecedented ways, the effort to have food and liquids legally defined as medical care has been accomplished in this country. Starvation and dehydration are presently becoming a widespread practice. This represents acceptance of voluntary and non-voluntary euthanasia (substituted judgment) both passive and active in character. How long will observing a loved one dying of starvation and dehydration be tolerated before humane and compassionate killing is prescribed?

To get a sense of the true purpose behind the move to sanction the removal of food and liquids from a patient, we should heed the words of Helga Kuhse. She is deputy director of the Centre for Human Bioethics at Monash University in Melbourne, Australia, and is a close associate of Peter Singer, the bioethicist who places a higher value on animals than on unborn children.

At a speech in 1984 to a gathering of euthanasia societies, Kuhse observed,

> If we can get people to accept the removal of all treatment and care—especially the removal of food and fluids—they will see what a painful way this is to die, and then, in the patient's best interest, they will accept the lethal injection.[4]

This trend has been accelerated in the United States because of the Nancy Cruzan case. As the result of a car accident, Nancy Cruzan had been in a persistent vegetative state since 11 January 1983. She was not brain dead and had been fed through a tube inserted in her stomach. Nurses who cared for her said she was awake, but not aware. They said she would turn toward persons when they spoke and had cried on several occasions.

Her parents went to court to have her feeding tube removed to allow her to die of starvation and dehydration. A state trial court ruled in the parent's favor, but the case was appealed to the Missouri State Supreme Court. The Missouri high court declared the need to err on the side of life and reversed the lower court decision.

The Missouri court correctly noted,

> [This is a] case in which euphemisms readily find their way into the fore, perhaps to soften the reality of what is really at stake. But this is not a case in which we are asked to let someone die. Nancy is not dead. Nor is she terminally ill. This is a case in which we are asked to allow the medical profession to make Nancy die by starvation and dehydration. The debate here is thus not between life and death; it is between quality of life and death.[5]

The parents would not accept this decision, and it was then sent to the U.S. Supreme Court for a final ruling. (I should note that the parents were not paying Nancy's medical bills; the state of Missouri was spending $130,000 a year to care for her, so it was not a financial burden that motivated them to end her life.)

On 25 June 1990, the court issued a decision upholding the Missouri Supreme Court decision. Unfortunately, this was not a real victory for the sanctity of life. The court held that because there was no way of knowing what Nancy Cruzan's wishes would be in this case, they

> ... rejected the argument that her parents were entitled to order the termination of her medical treatment, concluding that no person can assume that choice for an incompetent in the absence of the formalities required by the Living Will statute or clear and convincing evidence of the patient's wishes.[6]

What they did uphold, however, was the ultimate right of a patient to refuse not only medical treatment, but food and liquids as well, if they are competent or have expressed their desire to be starved/dehydrated to death if incapacitated. With this decision, the court included food and liquids as medical treatment.

What eventually happened to Nancy Cruzan? Her parents continued to gather circumstantial evidence that she would not have wanted to live in a persistent vegetative state, and in December 1990, her feeding tube was removed, and she died several days later.

A Reasonable Voice

In this U.S. Supreme Court decision, only Justice Antonin Scalia seems to have properly understood the significance of this case as it impacts human life. He noted, in part,

> The various opinions in this case portray quite clearly the difficult, indeed agonizing questions that are presented by the constantly increasing power of science to keep the human body alive for longer than any reasonable person would want to inhabit it. The States have begun to grapple with these problems through legislation. I am concerned, from the tenor of today's opinions, that we are poised to confuse that enter-

prise as successfully as we have confused that enterprise of legislating concerning abortion—requiring it to be conducted against a background of federal constitutional imperatives that are unknown because they are being newly crafted from Term to Term. That would be a great misfortune.

While I agree with the Court's analysis today, and therefore join in its opinion, I would have preferred that we announce, clearly and promptly, that the federal courts have no business in this field; that American law has always accorded the State power to prevent, by force if necessary, suicide—including suicide by refusing to take appropriate measures necessary to preserve one's life; that the point at which life becomes worthless, and the point at which the means necessary to preserve it become extraordinary, or inappropriate, are neither set forth in the Constitution nor known to the nine Justices of this Court any better than they are known to nine people picked at random from the Kansas City telephone directory; and hence, that even when it *is* demonstrated by clear and convincing evidence that a patient no longer wishes certain measures to be taken to preserve her life, it is up to the citizens of Missouri to decide, through their elected representatives, that that wish will be honored. It is quite impossible (because the Constitution says nothing about the matter) that those citizens will decide upon a line less lawful than the one we would choose; and it is unlikely (because we know no more about life-and-death than they do) that they will decide upon a line less reasonable.[7]

Nancy Cruzan's case is significant for a number of reasons, the primary reason being that this has legitimized the idea of starving and dehydrating a patient to death who is not terminally ill, is not dead, and requires no extraordinary measures to sustain life or control pain.

It also sets the stage for the next logical advance by pro-death doctors and euthanasia advocates to provide lethal injections or anesthesia to those who are being starved to death, to eliminate their suffering. Thus, we would normalize planned death—medicide—as standard medical practice.

The starvation of a person in a persistent vegetative state can also logically be extended to justify death solutions of others who are mentally ill, severely handicapped, senile, Alzheimer's victims, and fall into other categories of disabling and handicapping disorders.

In recognition of the sanctity of human life, no matter how fragile, the medical profession needs to resist the temptation to solve hard cases by compassionate killing. The effort should always be to control pain and provide comfort, care, and respect as the person goes through the natural dying process. We must distinguish between allowing to die and aid-in-dying.

The Doctor's Dilemma

In traditional medicine, the life and death issues were decided with a clear bias toward life, not toward the killing of the patient. Regrettably, the move toward patient autonomy has often impaired the ability of a doctor to provide proper care to a patient.

The passage of the Patient Self-Determination Act in December of 1991 by the U.S. Congress is a good example of the state meddling in what should be patient, family, and/or physician decisions. Under this act, states are required to pass rules and regulations dealing with the right of patients to give doctors so-called advanced directives as to the scope of medical care they receive in a hospital should they be incapacitated while undergoing surgery or other medical care. This law requires any health facility receiving federal money to put policies into place which require a person being admitted to the hospital to provide an advance directive.

On the surface, this sounds like a good idea. It provides the patient with the knowledge that no extraordinary measures will be used to keep him alive in an irreversible comatose or persistent vegetative state. The problem with this law is that it may limit the ability of a physician to make informed decisions about the kind of medical care a person should receive in a hospital. The advance directive basically inhibits the doctor from performing procedures or recommending medications which would possibly violate the advanced directive.

The use of the advanced directive is not necessarily the most effective way of discovering a patient's wishes. When a person enters the hospital for treatment, he is usually not thinking clearly about the possibilities or options. Informed consent is not really taking place because the patient has no way of knowing what the circumstances of his condition might be if he slips into a coma.

What this means is that the doctor may be inhibited from exercising his good judgment in seeking healing for the patient. He is bound to follow the advanced directive, even if the outcome may be ameliorated by active intervention. When and by what criteria are irreversible coma and PVS defined? By whom and under what constraints, implied or explicit?

How does this work out in practice? Let's take the fictional case of a Nancy Cruzan-like patient. She has already provided her physician with a living will giving instructions to allow her to be starved to death if she becomes comatose. Now she gets in a car wreck and enters the hospital in a coma, the physician is obligated by her advanced directive to follow through on her starvation, even though he may have some hope for her recovery.

If the doctor insists on treatment and sustenance out of humanitarian concern for her value as a person, he is at risk of a lawsuit brought by angry parents or guardians. Additionally, he may be censured by administrators should the coma later become irreversible and large sums have been expended in providing long-term treatment and care.

This situation gets even more bizarre. I'm familiar with one actual case involving a nursing home and the parents of a person who was incapacitated. The parents wanted the hospital to allow her to die by cessation of sustenance. The hospital staff decided it would be more appropriate for the patient if she were sent home. The parents, however, didn't want to see her die at home; they preferred to have her starved to death at a nursing home facility. When the facility administrators refused to perform this service, the parents sued and won $160 million.

A hospital should not be a holding facility for coma or PVS victims; nor should a hospital staff committed to active treatment and rehabilitation be forced to starve patients against hospital and staff wishes. Needless to say, few nursing homes are willing to deliberately starve their patients to death. As the pro-death movement gains more legal victories in courts and legislatures, and the need to control health care costs becomes obsessive, a trend will be established to sanction aid-in-dying—active euthanasia.

The doctor also faces an additional dilemma because of the Patient Self-Determination Act. What if the patient's advance directive requires the doctor to provide medical care far beyond a reasonable limit for someone who is dying? In traditional medical practice, the doctor is not ethically bound to prolong the dying process, or continue futile efforts to keep someone alive who is obviously terminally ill. Yet this advanced directive policy impedes the physician's judgment in this instance also.

The third party insurer, a court decision, a federal or state policy—all of these tend to impair the ability of a doctor to provide proper care to his patient. What once used to be a close bond between doctor and patient has been effectively severed by interfering third parties.

It saddens me to see the breaking of this bond between patient, family, and doctor. There used to be an ethos of trust and care between the parties that is rare in modern medicine. The doctor too often looks at the patient as simply an illness to be overcome, not as a person with an illness. The illness, not the individual, is the thing to be healed. This broken relationship will only continue to deteriorate if the ethos of death as a solution permeates the medical profession.

How will the patient feel when he is confronted with a doctor who sees no clearly defined difference between healing or killing the patient? Can you imagine lying in a hospital bed and being visited by a pro-death physician? How would you react if he asked you how you were doing and then said, "Would you like to live a few more years, or shall we plan your death?" You probably wouldn't have much confidence in his dedication to healing you. You would be right to question whether he really has your best interest at heart.

The Living Will and Durable Power of Attorney

Personally, I would not sign a living will because one really doesn't know what one's condition will be when one is incapacitated. In my opinion, a far better way of handling these decisions in the event you're incapacitated is through a durable power of attorney. Decisions concerning life and death require a trust, a covenantal relationship, and is best managed by a family member, associate, or friend designated to act in your best interest.

The durable power of attorney is a grant of authority to a trusted individual. It can be a blanket grant of authority or you can be more specific. The person who is given this authority has a degree of latitude in decision-making in consultation with your doctor.

The International Anti-Euthanasia Task Force (IAETF) has produced what it calls a Protective Medical Decisions Document (PMDD) which could provide you with a measure of safety should you become incapacitated. As Rita Marker, the director of the IAETF, explains in her introduction to the PMDD,

> It had always been traditional for a family member to make decisions if a patient was unable to do so. This is rapidly changing. Legally, a family member is not automatically an adult patient's guardian.

Killing as Medical Treatment

In fact, recent cases make it clear that medical providers are now willing to go to court to have strangers appointed to make decisions to withdraw care against the wishes of the patient and a capable, loving family.

The Protective Medical Decisions Document specifically defines and prohibits euthanasia and it instructs that you will be given ordinary nursing and medical care, including pain relief and provided sustenance, food and liquids.

Rita Marker notes that this form of protection is far better than a living will because the living will is a vague declaration that takes rights and control from its signer and gives decision-making authority to a physician (who may not even know the patient). A living will also gives a physician complete immunity from civil or criminal liability for his or her actions or inactions. (Information about the International Anti-Euthanasia Task Force is provided in the appendix.)

The Death Initiatives in California and Washington

As noted earlier in this chapter, the Hemlock Society has been active in promoting aid-in-dying legislation in a number of states in recent years. In 1992, voters in California narrowly defeated a Hemlock-supported ballot initiative that would have allowed physician-assisted suicide. The initiative was actively promoted by Americans Against Human Suffering, founded by attorney Robert L. Risley.

The initiative, if passed, would have allowed voluntary euthanasia where the patient could request to have the doctor kill him. Risley's proposal supposedly contained a number of procedural safeguards which he listed as follows:

1. Competent adults should have the right to request and receive physician aid in dying when they are terminally ill;

2. Physicians should be protected from criminal, civil

and administrative liability if they comply with the patient's request;

3. The request should be in the form of a written directive, with two disinterested parties prepared in advance of the terminal condition;

4. The prognosis should be independently confirmed by a second physician and that upon the request of a competent patient to a treating physician, the physician would comply;

5. The physician compliance would be voluntary, not compulsory.

Fortunately, a coalition of churches, the California Medical Society, the American Cancer Society, and other groups joined forces to aggressively oppose this Death With Dignity Act in California.

David Llewellyn, founder of the Western Center for Law and Religious Freedom in Sacramento, California, wrote an incisive analysis of the Death With Dignity Act and distributed thousands of copies throughout the state in an effort to defeat the pro-death initiative. According to Llewellyn, the Death with Dignity Act

> is barbaric evidence of the regression of American culture and values. Suicide cannot cure anything, for individuals or societies. If people's lives have lost meaning, the remedy is not to murder them, with or without their permission, but to restore the meaning to their lives.
>
> A society which abandons people who have given up on themselves has relinquished the right to call itself a society. Like armies that shoot their wounded, whatever cause or ideals they were fighting for have already been destroyed.[8]

The initiative proposed in Washington state in 1991 was similarly flawed. Dr. Robin Bernhoft, founder of Washington Physicians Against 119 (the initiative number which would have legalized killing), notes that the aid-in-dying legislation would have legalized two things: doctor-assisted suicide, in which the patient takes a fatal dose of a prescribed drug, or *direct euthanasia* in which the doctor or a health care worker gives the patient medicine, usually an injection, to stop the heart or respiration.[9]

Under 119, no safeguards were in place. If passed, this law would have allowed any physician armed with a second opinion to kill a patient. The doctor would not have had to provide any treatment options such as pain control, treatment alternatives, or psychiatric counseling.

The educational battle to defeat Initiative 119 was not an easy one. The pro-death group, Washington Citizens for Death With Dignity, had been able to gather more than a million signatures to put the issue on the ballot.

Bernhoft and a coalition of pro-life groups eventually came together, assigning functions and duties, in a coordinated effort to educate the public as to the dangers of the initiative. Polling was conducted to determine what kind of message would be presented to the public. To Bernhoft's surprise, the polling showed that the idea of frightening people with the specter of doctors killing their patients would have been ineffective. People had apparently been conditioned to believe that killing was rational and justifiable if good enough reasons were presented or it was determined that it was the person's choice.

What did frighten people, however, was their realization that *any* doctor could provide aid-in-dying to (kill) his patient; that no family notification was required; that litigation could result, splitting families; that poor people without health insurance might be more likely to choose death than others; that there was no waiting period or psychiatric review; and that the Dutch experience demonstrated that involuntary euthanasia and *crypthanasia* (hidden euthanasia) would be the next inevitable step in the process.

We can be somewhat encouraged that the California and Washington state efforts were defeated, but the battle continues to protect the sanctity of life from those who are determined to legalize killing as medical services provided to those exercising their autonomous right to choice-in-dying.

As a physician who believes in the sanctity of human life, I cannot simply remain silent as the doctors of death continue to push killing as good medical practice.

Hospice Care

It is not sufficient to simply oppose the passage of laws which would legalize the killing of patients. There must be a positive response to the issue of how we deal with terminally ill individuals, those in a persistent vegetative state, and those suffering from chronic disease and disorders, especially those experiencing uncontrolled pain.

One of the most effective ways of helping those at risk is the hospice movement, first pioneered in England.

The National Hospice Organization defines the hospice philosophy in these words:

> Hospice affirms life. Hospice exists to provide support and care for persons in the last phases of incurable disease so that they might live as fully and comfortably as possible. Hospice recognizes dying as a normal process whether or not resulting from disease.
>
> Hospice neither hastens nor postpones death. Hospice exists in the hope and belief that, through appropriate care and the promotion of a caring community sensitive to their needs, patients and families may be free to attain a degree of mental and spiritual preparation for death that is satisfactory to them.[10]

One strong advocate of the hospice movement in the U.S. is Dr. David Cundiff, an oncologist and hospice care physician practicing in California. Writing in his recently published book, *Euthanasia is NOT the Answer*, Cundiff explains the dangers of euthanasia and urges his readers to actively support the hospice concept and palliative care.

Dr. Cundiff became an advocate of hospice care after going to England in 1979 to study the movement there. What he learned shocked him.

> I had no idea that my pain management skills were grossly lacking. *I didn't know that I didn't know how to treat cancer pain* because I had rarely seen it done successfully.[11]

Cundiff notes that in England nearly 80 percent of the hospice patients are pain-free, or suffer only mild pain. They remain alert and often stay at home until they die.

The management of pain is a key element in providing compassionate care for terminally ill patients. If pain is managed effectively, there is no legitimate reason for physicians to kill their patients. As Dr. Cundiff says,

> We have the knowledge and the means to assure that no terminally ill person need beg for death to end his or her suffering. . . . Universally available, excellent quality hospice medicine is the life-affirming alternative to the hopelessness of euthanasia.[12]

Chapter 8

AIDS:
Killing by Medical Neglect

The morally bankrupt philosophy and ethic of radical autonomy—combined with the idea that individuals have an absolute right to unrestrained sexual expression—has become firmly established.

This has resulted in a disastrous public health response to the spread of HIV, the virus that causes AIDS. In an exaggerated concern and fear of discrimination engendered by gay activists, public health officials, politicians, and other opinion leaders, the AIDS epidemic has been allowed to flourish almost unhindered in the United States. As a result of a misplaced hysteria over discrimination, gays, bisexuals, IV drug users, prostitutes, hemophiliacs as well as heterosexuals, have died and are dying by the thousands.

Instead of implementing standard health procedures to control the spread of a lethal sexually transmitted disease, our public health officials have neglected their obligation to protect the health of the communities they are to serve. Playing an important role in the delay of applying standard health measures is the gay rights movement. Their cries of persecution, discrimination, and alienation from society have resulted in the establishment of numerous policies which ensure the continued spread of HIV/AIDS within the high risk communities.

As a former public health official, both in the federal government and at the state level in Florida, I have witnessed first hand how foolish these policies are and how homosexual activists have enhanced the spread of the epidemic by opposing proven public health infectious disease procedures.

The Public Health Service Response to Drugs and AIDS

My first experience in the public health service came in November of 1986, when I was appointed director of the U.S. government's Office of Substance Abuse and Prevention in the Department of Health and Human Services. This new office was a creation of the Congress in response to growing concern over the use of drugs and alcohol among our nation's youth. Our mandate was to develop and implement primary prevention efforts to stem substance abuse among the nation's teen-agers.

This program was part of the Public Health Service under the Alcohol, Drug Abuse and Mental Health Administration (ADAMHA) which included the National Institute for Drug Abuse (NIDA), the National Institute of Mental Health (NIMH), and the National Institute of Alcohol and Alcoholism (NIAA). Other components of the federal public health effort includes the Food and Drug Administration (FDA), the Centers for Disease Control (CDC), the Health Resources and Services Administration (HRSA), and the National Institutes of Health (NIH).

All of these various agencies were developing separate programs to deal with their specific areas of expertise, and my office was provided with resources, personnel, and staff assistance from a number of these bureaucracies. My immediate supervisor was Dr. Ian McDonald, a fellow pediatrician who had moved to Washington, D.C., from Clearwater, Florida, to help guide the Reagan administration's "war on drugs." Our job was to promote primary prevention programs nationwide that would convince non-drug-using teens to avoid initiating drug use. Also, secondary prevention programs (early intervention) to attain non-use by drug-using teens and tertiary prevention to provide early treatment and rehabilitation.

My experience in the Office of Substance Abuse was a difficult but rewarding experience that resulted in positive programs and outcomes. Other than understanding the workings of a governmental bureaucracy, the singular value of this year was the clear recognition that primary prevention—changing behavior—was necessary to attain good health, for our youth in particular. Their lack of self-control and health-harmful behavior can be attributed to the preceding breakdown in family life, especially the absence of fathers in the home.

Tracking Teen Promiscuity and AIDS

Once back in Florida, I became medical director of the Escambia County Public Health Unit, serving the Pensacola area. I also worked as the medical director of the Children's Medical Services for the westernmost four-county area of the Florida panhandle. As a public health officer, it was my responsibility to do whatever I could to protect the health of the community I was serving. As a public health officer and a pediatrician, my greatest concern remains the prevention of health harmful behaviors.

The basic principle of public health services is *prevention* and its three elements: primary, secondary, and tertiary prevention. The first concern is **Primary Prevention**. This involves conducting educational programs to convince at-risk groups to refrain from health-harmful sexual and drug behavior and environmenal control in eliminating infectious disease, toxic exposure, and reducing injury. My work in developing the drug prevention programs in the federal government proved useful. As a pediatrician, my goal is to convince patients to refrain from or to stop behaviors that will hurt or perhaps kill them—which includes health education and motivation.

Secondary Prevention involves early intervention to minimize the harmful risk behavior that can result from exposure to drug use, infectious agents, toxic chemicals, or other destructive health practices. The goal is to minimize the harm and eliminate the harmful factor. A good example is smoking cessation. Primary prevention is to persuade individuals to never start smoking, while secondary prevention is to persuade the smoker to stop smoking and to sustain a non-smoking status.

Tertiary Prevention involves treatment and rehabilitation of the individual injured by health-harmful behavior—for example, minimizing dysfunction and progression of the smoking-induced disease or disorder, e.g., chronic lung disease.

All of these elements of prevention are designed to prevent the risk behavior and to ameliorate the harmful effects of infectious disease, substance abuse, toxic exposure and injury.

As a public health officer, the major focus is on the primary prevention of infectious diseases, sexually transmitted diseases, HIV/AIDS, hepatitis, unwanted pregnancy, etc., and to provide access to health care for those in need. I became particularly involved in monitoring the spread of HIV infection and AIDS in a four-county area of Florida. It soon became evident that our response to the epidemic was grossly inadequate.

The standard public health procedures to control this epidemic of an infectious disease, spread primarily by intimate sexual exposure and IV drug use, were not implemented due to the political barriers which essentially designated the disease as a handicap in order to prevent discrimination against those infected.

Standard procedures would include the following:

1. **Adequate Testing** to determine and track the numbers and demographics of individuals infected.

2. **Partner Elicitation and Contact Tracing**, an interviewing process identifying sexual partners and/or IV

drug users sharing needles and syringes with the infected individual.

3. **Partner Notification** of those exposed to the infected carrier in order to test. If negative, the individual is educated to avoid exposure; if positive, he/she is given treatment and directions as to prevention in spreading the disease further.

4. **Isolation and Monitoring** is recommended for those who knowingly continue to infect others; monitoring is designed to discourage infected individuals from participation in high risk sex and drug behaviors in order to minimize HIV transmission.

These are the proven traditional steps that are taken in identifying and controlling the spread of infectious diseases, such as tuberculosis, hepatitis, syphilis, and other sexually transmitted diseases.

These routine infectious disease control procedures have been modified by complicated and time-consuming procedural requirements in providing informed consent, pre- and post-test counseling, stringent confidentiality rules and regulations, stiff penalties for breaks in consent and confidentiality procedures and restrictions as to reporting and the use of testing data. This has resulted in limited testing, largely confined to targeted high risk populations (STD clinics, prison inmates, prostitutes, and IV drug users, etc.) Anonymous testing centers have been established in the community along with confidential testing centers primarily based in public health facilities. Sero-prevalence surveys are periodically done on select populations (neonatal, pre-natal women) and routinely periodic testing is done in the armed forces.

The consequence is that private physicians as well as hospitals, clinics, emergency rooms, and other health care settings are encumbered and reluctant to test even upon clinical indications. Additionally, laboratory results of HIV positive tests are not routinely reportable and only those HIV+ patients who develop AIDS are reported. AIDS surveillance workers often have to review death certificates and other indirect avenues in attempting to ascertain the incidence and prevalence of HIV infection and AIDS.

In effect, due to the political influence of the gay activist lobby and their supporters, effective, proven infectious disease control methods are restricted while the epidemic proceeds apace. Ironically, the homosexual community and IV drug users (commonly involved in exchange of drugs for sex) are the overwhelming victims of a miserable, lethal, infectious disease.

HIV/AIDS is being managed as a totally different category of disease under current state and federal laws. As a result of redefinition, those who have HIV/AIDS are euphemistically considered handicapped and protected from discrimination. Meanwhile, ineffective education programs featuring condom use do little or nothing to change the high risk behavior that causes the spread of the disease into the population at large.

Why Is a Virus Politically Protected?

The history of the HIV/AIDS epidemic in the United States provides an understanding of how the gay activists and their consorts have managed to distort the issue of a primary unhealthy, high risk behavior, i.e., anal sex.

The advent of the so-called Gay-Related Immunodeficiency Syndrome (GRID) in 1981 prompted a huge effort by the Centers for Disease Control (CDC), the National Institutes of Health, and medical researchers to determine the etiology (or cause) of AIDS. By 1985, the etiology was established. The gay community, from the inception of the epidemic, realized that HIV/AIDS could seriously undermine their efforts to gain acceptance, not simply tolerance, of homosexuality as a normal alternative life-style, no different than heterosexual relationships.

They declared HIV/AIDS everybody's disease and projected its rapid sexual spread into the heterosexual population. This stampeded a disproportionate allocation of health research funding to HIV/AIDS in the desperate hope of finding a vaccine or effective drug therapy. The heterosexual spread of the disease in this country (not in the third world) is being confined by changed behavior and will continue to primarily afflict the high risk groups of homosexuals, bisexuals, and IV drug users. The gay activists strategize that the HIV/AIDS epidemic could be of significant benefit to them in developing educational materials designed to normalize the behavior and establish a victim status, garnering sympathy for those infected and dying of AIDS. Far from being a hindrance to gay rights, the AIDS epidemic has proven to be an economic gold mine and an opportunity to legitimize their life-style. Federal and state grant monies have poured into their coffers, allowing the gays to virtually control the response to the AIDS epidemic and direct the sex education curricula and attain teaching roles in the massive movement for comprehensive health education.

Gay activists and their supporters convinced politicians that standard infectious disease control measures would be discriminatory against gays as a class. They convinced politicians and public health officials that if HIV/AIDS were treated routinely as a sexually transmitted disease, those infected would be driven underground and refuse to be tested because of fear of gay-bashing. Soft policies on dealing with the epidemic were instituted.

As a result of these policies, the epidemic has spread virtually uncontrolled through the gay population, IV drug users, prostitutes and hemophiliacs and now it places the heterosexual population at risk, especially our adolescents and youth.

The best hope and primary prevention—ceasing sodomy—was rejected. The idea of trying to educate the homosexual population into changing the dangerous behaviors associated with anal sex was considered unrealistic. The pro-gay policy-makers judged that this population should have the right to engage in high risk behaviors, regardless of the effect it might have on themselves, others, or on our health care system. The emphasis was misplaced on the safe sex and then safer sex message to reduce the risk of transmission per sexual encounter. The condom became the ultimate weapon in the fight against AIDS. Meanwhile, sodomy, the crucial high risk behavior continues unabated.

Former Surgeon General C. Everett Koop was embroiled in this controversy back in the mid-1980s when he issued a national report on the AIDS epidemic. He recommended monogamy in marriage and condom use only as a way of reducing the rate of spread of the disease among those who engaged in high risk sexual behaviors. The condom, however, has been of relatively little value in halting the spread of HIV/AIDS by anal sex and has undermined the primary prevention principle of ceasing the high risk behavior.

Regrettably, the condom continues to be touted as the solution to the AIDS epidemic. The advocacy of safer sex is not only naive but dangerous to those who think that a thin layer of latex will protect one from a fatal disease. As Dr. Joe McIlhaney points out in his book, *Sexuality and Sexually Transmitted Diseases*, at least 10 to 20 percent of condoms have manufacturing defects in them.[1]

In addition, the advocates of condom use routinely fail to tell their audiences that the AIDS virus is about fifty times smaller than the usual hole that passes inspection in an intact condom. A sperm is 45 microns in size; a typical hole in a condom is approximately 5 microns in size, but the AIDS virus is 0.1 microns in size.[2] The safety of condoms in protecting people from HIV/AIDS transmission in anal sex was rather dramatically debunked in 1987 when a federally subsidized study in Los Angeles was cancelled because it posed too great a danger to those who would be involved.

Why do many sex educators continue health education curriculum that promote condoms along with anal intercourse as normative for protection against HIV/AIDS? They do it because it is part of the gay agenda to present homosexuality as a legitimate life-style to our teen-agers. Under the guise of HIV/AIDS education, pro-gay educators have unlimited access to our children and teens to teach them about oral and anal sex along with condom use. It seems to matter little to them that they are dooming many to HIV/AIDS infection and a miserable, painful death. It is truly incredible that a lethal, epidemic, sexually transmitted viral infection such as HIV/AIDS, which is primarily spread by anal sex, is assigned a faulty latex shield while the high risk sexual behavior is depicted as normative, not warranting any limits.

The Progression of the Disease

Since the safer sex message was adopted as official policy in this country in 1987, we have seen the tragic and continued spread of HIV/AIDS throughout the high risk populations. There is no primary emphasis on changing behavior to eliminate the risk of infection; the emphasis is on secondary prevention (condoms) that simply delays or reduces the risk of death. This is considered realistic by those who oversee AIDS policies in this country. Personally, I think it is unconscionable and a dereliction of duty for public health officials to recommend policies that fail to control the epidemic. Because of these foolish policies, far more people have unnecessarily died of AIDS than would have if we had only followed our standard health procedures. What of the rights of the uninfected?

Today, we still do not have good data on how widespread this disease has become in our society. It has been estimated that for every one person that we know has AIDS, another ten to twenty may have it. Remarkably, it is estimated that only one of ten persons who are HIV infected know they are infected.

In addition, we have drastically underestimated the spread of this disease because of the way our public health officials have defined HIV/AIDS. Under current definitions, a person who is found to have HIV infection is not considered to have AIDS. He is only counted as a statistic when he comes down with a physical ailment that is part of the criteria for the AIDS definition. This arbitrary definition hides the true extent of the AIDS epidemic because it fails to include all those individuals who test positive for HIV. These individuals are symptomatic yet infectious. They are not ill and most likely (ten to one odds) do not know they are infectious.

We do not separate carriers of syphilis into two different categories: those who have the syphilis spirochete and those who have symptoms of syphilis. The person who has the spirochete has the disease. There is no logical reason for HIV to be separated from AIDS. It is one and the same disease, only different stages. All individuals who have HIV infection should be counted in statistics because given time, almost all will develop full blown AIDS.

It is a dreadful fact that an estimated nine out of ten people in this country who have HIV, don't realize it because they have not been tested. With current policies protecting gays from potential discrimination, there is no incentive for these people to find out if they are infected or to stop infecting others. The current restrictive policies are so rigidly drawn as to prevent effective tracking of the spread of the disease. The rules of counseling, consent, and reporting are so strict that a physician who may have a need to know tends to defer testing of his patient. With HIV being considered a disability or handicap, common sense tracking procedures will continue to be ignored and more people will die unnecessarily. The availability of improved treatment creates a need to know for the infected individual. This serves as further warrant for more adequate testing.

Developing Separate Clinics for AIDS Treatment

In failing to treat HIV/AIDS as a sexually transmitted disease, the public health officials of this country have established separate clinics to deal only with AIDS patients. Several years ago, Congress passed a law creating the Ryan White Fund to help establish AIDS clinics throughout the country. This funding was designated to state public health offices who in turn would identify community-based organizations to set up and run AIDS clinics.

As a public health officer, it was my job to help identify and support these groups in the Pensacola area. They were to develop HIV/AIDS support groups, anonymous testing (no identity) sites, and case management services for those with AIDS and their families.

My role was to provide competent medical personnel, including a physician, nurses, and case management that would make certain that HIV/AIDS patients received proper medical care. These community-based clinics were independently operated, although I retained accountability and oversight for the medical services involved.

I also worked closely with the local medical society, their infectious disease specialists, hospitals, and other medical care facilities to coordinate access to good medical care for HIV/AIDS patients. As a member of the local county medical society's AIDS Task Force, I worked with physicians an hospitals to make sure that AIDS patients received needed medical care, drugs and laboratory procedures, emergency room care, and hospitalization.

Unfortunately, during my time overseeing these services, it became obvious that the lack of adequate prevention was thwarting efforts to effectively deal with the epidemic. Gay activists lobbying influence made certain no laws or regulations were imposed that would enable effective surveillance or control.

The gay activists and their political allies may have succeeded in preventing some discrimination, but they have done so at the expense of thousands of lives and untold pain to those who have lost their loved ones to this disease. One group that has been most unfairly harmed by bad public policy measures dealing with HIV/AIDS are the nation's hemophiliacs. These sufferers have been decimated by infected blood products, contributing a tragic chapter to medical history, and one that should never be allowed to occur again.

The blame for the lack of adequate control of this epidemic lies squarely on the shoulders of gay rights activists and the misplaced, unrealistic sympathy of politicians, public health officials, and physicians who have protected HIV/AIDS from standard infectious disease control measures. They have protected the right of infected individuals to be promiscuously sexually active, endangering the lives of thousands of people—all on the premise that to limit sexual expression would destroy a person's liberty or the freedom to autonomously choose to be sexually promiscuous in any fashion as a matter of their individual right to privacy. This does harm to others and society. Sexuality may be practiced in private, but it is profoundly a social issue.

During my stay as public health officer, I noticed a growing disillusionment among other physicians over the AIDS epidemic. They felt that they were hindered in their ability to control the disease. Many of them tended to shy away from treating AIDS patients because of the constraints placed upon them. It took a great effort to convince physicians to continue giving care to AIDS patients.

As I have observed the progression of this epidemic, it has become obvious to me that there will be a growing need for community-based responses to AIDS. The HIV/AIDS patient's condition is so complex, and the social needs are so great, that it is essential that communities develop a broadly based medical, social support system to care for them in the various stages of the dying process. It has been estimated, conservatively, that one AIDS patient's care costs $80,000 a year, though this figure is decreasing due to new techniques in management. The HIV/AIDS clinics and their support groups are in desperate need of compassionate volunteers to work with those who are dying of this dreadful disease, and their hurting families.

Adolescents at Risk

With the current inadequate safer sex message being taught to our children, it is unlikely that this epidemic will subside or be controlled in the near future. Promoting condom use as a way of preventing infection while condoning anal intercourse as legitimate sexual behavior will undoubtedly lead to a surge in adolescent infections during the next few years.

While I was working in the public health service in Florida, condom-mania became rampant, yet no serious or significant efforts were being made to encourage abstinence as a way of eliminating unwanted pregnancies, sexually transmitted diseases, or HIV/AIDS.

It is bad medical practice for doctors and sex educators to be teaching condom use as safe, instead of teaching teens to use self control in abstaining from sexual activities until they are married. The attitude seems to be that no health official should ever presume to abridge a teen's alleged right to sexual expression, as if nothing could be more important in the world than for a young person to experience early intercourse.

The fact of the matter is that HIV/AIDS will kill the teen just as effectively as it kills the IV drug user, the bisexual, the homosexual, and the prostitute. The honest, caring message we should give our teens is that premarital, promiscuous sex has the potential of killing them via a long and painful process if they are infected with the HIV/AIDS virus.

Gays, of course, recognize the fact that a majority of their population will eventually die of AIDS. It then becomes essential to recruit new members into the life-style. The questions we should ask are these: Have they targeted vulnerable youth (waverers in their sexual identity) for recruitment? Have they been targeted not only through AIDS curricula, but through other areas such as social sciences, literature, the media, and multicultural studies?

My greatest concern is for the young, adventurous adolescent males who have an unrealistic sense of immortality. These young men are placing themselves at considerable risk as they experiment with premarital and promiscuous sex either through homosexual liaisons or encounters with prostitutes who may be HIV positive. As the numbers of sexual partners increase, the risk for infection increases dramatically.

What Needs to be Done?

We in the medical profession desperately need to return to standard infectious disease control measures to bring the HIV/AIDS epidemic under control within the high risk groups while minimizing its spread into the rest of the population. The American people have enough experience and education. We should institute routine testing for HIV infection upon principled medical indication, which could be based upon a patient's medical history or when he has a physical exam. This information can be handled confidentially by health professionals as we do other infectious and sexually transmitted disease situations. The society can and would provide compassionate care even while disagreeing with and discouraging the harmful sex and drug behavior.

Partner elicitation and contact tracing is needed in order to provide early intervention with treatment that is available and to prevent known carriers from infecting others. This effort would undoubtedly be protested by gay activists and their sexual license apologists and cohorts in the straight population, but the fact is that these measures are needed to protect these individuals from themselves as well as others, and the community from an infection that brings on certain death. The gays, unfortunately, will not tolerate the concept that their behavior might be immoral or ultimately unhealthy. They believe fervently that they have a right to acceptance (not mere tolerance) and the absolute right to sexual freedom no matter what the cost may be to themselves and to others. This hedonistic and selfish attitude should not be allowed to drive our public health response to this epidemic.

We should change laws and regulations at the federal and state level to properly define HIV and its later stage, AIDS, as the same disease and to define it as a homosexually and heterosexually transmitted disease, not as a handicap.

We need wider routine testing, particularly among high risk groups, to track the spread of the disease. This should be done routinely for the benefit of the patient and for society as a whole. These test results should be reportable so that we will have adequate epidemiological knowledge of the incidence and prevalence of the epidemic.

We should institute aggressive partner elicitation, tracing, and notification programs as we routinely do for tuberculosis and other infectious diseases. In partner elicitation, we should do whatever we can to convince the person infected to notify those he may have infected so that they can obtain early treatment. If he refuses, then the health care worker may notify the person infected on a confidential basis to encourage him to get help as well as notifying those he may have infected. Modifying and/ or ceasing the high risk behavior is a reasonable expectation in stopping the spread of HIV/AIDS. This is the truly caring and compassionate response to this infection. In spite of the current irrational passion for radical autonomy and the so-called right to choice, we should place reasonable constraints on those who knowingly spread the disease. This will involve rational persuasion and discrimination in the best interest of others and the community. This disease is harmful. It causes harm to others and to the community.

Irresponsible behavior by a carrier of HIV infection is unacceptable and warrants personal, moral, social, and legal constraints. These constraints might be confinement (in a hospital or clinic) or monitoring of the person's behavior as we commonly do for parolees. Public health departments quite often monitor the activities of prostitutes who are spreading syphilis or other venereal diseases, as well as drug abusers. After spending time in jail, the prostitute will often be assigned a worker who monitors the woman's behavior to assure adequate treatment and to prevent further spread of disease.

It is irrational to assume that individuals who knowingly spread a lethal disease should be free of constraints. The person who has HIV/AIDS and knowingly places another individual at risk has assaulted that person as surely as if he had hit him in the head.

The claims of the right to freedom of sexual expression ring hollow when a person is going to die as a result of risky sexual behavior. No civilized society can afford to tolerate sexual license in the name of sexual freedom—especially when sickness and death result from the activity.

Contrary to what gay activists or ACLU libertarians would have you believe, all of us in society are accountable to one another for our behavior. The drunk driver who kills a child is held accountable for his behavior; the gang member who slashes the throat of a neighbor is held accountable for his actions; the drug pusher who sells cocaine to elementary school children is held accountable for his actions; and the AIDS carrier who knowingly infects another should be held accountable as well.

In Boston, New York, and other major cities, hospitals are now detaining individuals who are spreading a new and dangerous strain of tuberculosis. Although the authorities are reluctant to do so, they are compelled to detain these individuals in order to protect the public health and safety. In Boston, Lemuel Shattuck Hospital has detained fifteen individuals during the last two years. In New York City, forty TB patients were detained in 1991, and Los Angeles has jailed several.[3]

The new strain of drug-resistant TB began appearing in the mid-1980s and has been linked with the spread of HIV/AIDS. In New York City, for example, the annual number of TB cases jumped from 1,514 to 3,520, with a 30 percent increase in 1990 alone. In November 1991,

TB killed thirteen people in New York prisons. Twelve of those individuals were HIV positive. A prison guard who had been assigned to guard four of these prisoners also contracted TB and later died.

Drug resistant TB is spreading among AIDS carriers in New York and in Miami. And of course, San Francisco has a TB rate five times as great as the city associated with the HIV/AIDS epidemic and promiscuous sex.[4] In Los Angeles, health officials are detaining at least two individuals each month to prevent them from spreading tuberculosis. They stay in jail from two weeks up to 180 days.[5]

Surely these same health measures could also be applied to HIV/AIDS carriers, especially those who knowingly infect other individuals. In Colorado, efforts have been made to enforce constraints against those who knowingly infect others with AIDS. Laws enacted in 1985 and 1987 provide for a positive, but still somewhat flawed response to the AIDS epidemic. According to El Paso County health officials, in a recent article entitled, "Restricting Personal Behavior: case studies on legal measures to prevent the spread of HIV" in the *International Journal of STD and AIDS*, the Colorado laws provide that

> Health officers in Colorado can require a person with HIV-infection to receive counselling, and may order an infected person to cease and desist from conduct which endangers others. If necessary, they may enforce those orders by restricting specific behaviors. Infected people who recklessly or intentionally endanger others are also subject to criminal prosecution.[6]

In El Paso County, which encompasses Colorado Springs and surrounding communities, the health department has encountered at least twenty HIV-infected people who knew they were infected and knowingly exposed others to the virus. At least two more individuals became infected. The authors note that many HIV-infected people cannot accept the fact that they are infected; others are careless or negligent; drug abuse or AIDS dementia may cloud their judgment.

The laws providing for mandatory counseling and monitoring, however, are flawed because of the extended appeal and legal process that must be followed. As the El Paso County health officers note, "Disturbingly, these statutes permit an individual to expose others repeatedly; a person who ignores all entreaties has at least 5 opportunities to spread the virus before court sanctions are available."[7] They advise that criminal law, independent of public health efforts, was swifter and more effective in dealing with those who knowingly infect others. Despite some of the flaws in the Colorado laws, they could be used as models for other states to adopt in controlling the behavior of those who willingly infect others.

As part of a sound public health policy designed to control the spread of HIV/AIDS, we should make every effort to maintain laws against anal sodomy. Anal intercourse is still the most common means of transmitting AIDS to others. It is against all common sense and decency for our nation to be decriminalizing or removing sodomy laws when the AIDS epidemic is readily spread by anal intercourse.

Why would a sane society remove social and legal barriers to a behavior that will kill millions of individuals? The HIV/AIDS epidemic hurts not only the person infected, but others and society in general. In the interests of the society at large, and individuals not yet infected, we must maintain and strengthen our sodomy laws in order to discourage an unhealthy and potentially lethal behavior. We should demand that sodomy laws be kept in place even if they are not aggressively enforced against private, consensual behavior. We should do this because the law is a standard that draws the line on behavior that is not considered healthy or normative by our society.

Under no circumstances should we tolerate the continued spread of HIV/AIDS by those who are too irresponsible to use self control. These individuals should not be protected by a health system or a life-style establishment that condones knowingly infected individuals infecting others with a lethal disease.

As compassionate killing and a presumed right to die gains acceptance in medicine, I foresee the promotion of a presumed right to suicide for AIDS patients. Kevorkian's medicide—planned death—could be used to eliminate the suffering of AIDS patients, including homosexuals, IV drug users, and prostitutes who have been infected.

Chapter 9

Bioethics and the New Pagans

The starvation of Baby Doe in 1982 with parent, physician, and court approval proved to be a clarion call for those of us in the medical profession who were concerned about bioethical issues. As a reaction against the possibility that the medical profession would normalize infanticide, a number of medical and legal groups sprang up to deal with medical ethical dilemmas and new philosophical theories in ethics. Both the federal government and a number of foundations came forward with grant money to fund bioethical think tanks to deal with future Baby Doe cases and other similar ethical cases.

The new technologies which had been developed in the 1970s presented physicians with ethical dilemmas they'd never encountered before. Once the Baby Doe case was widely debated, it became obvious that bioethical training was going to be an essential element in the education of a physician.

Bioethical think tanks sprang up in New York, Minnesota, California, and in hospitals like Johns Hopkins and Houston's Texas Medical Center. The Kennedy Institute at Georgetown University became one of the better known bioethics centers.

However, the most prominent secular bioethics think tank is the Hastings Center based in Hastings-on-the Hudson, New York. The founder of the Hastings Center is Dr. Will Gaylin, and Daniel Callahan is its primary ethics spokesman. An organization which has established itself as a defender of the right to life is the National Center for the Medically Dependent and Disabled, Inc., in association with the Horatio R. Storer Foundation, a not-for-profit group that publishes books on medical and legal issues. The National Center's publication, *Issues in Law and Medicine*, presents both the pros and cons of current bioethical controversies.

Effective pro-life think tanks were also established at a number of Catholic universities, including Catholic University in Washington, D.C., and the Pope Pius Center in St. Louis. The religious-based bioethics groups gave voice to theism and the transcendent meaning of the lives of human beings. They championed the sanctity of life ethic as opposed to the secularist quality of life ethic espoused by Joseph Fletcher and others. These think tanks developed research publications and provided training to physicians, medical students, lawyers, and other influential members of our society as to bio-social and medical matters. However, the secularist viewpoint and their think tanks have dominated the debate with their humanistic, materialist, utilitarian viewpoint where God's existence is moot and the functional value of individuals, their quality of life, is the overriding principle.

Two World Views Collide

Widely divergent views have developed in the field of bioethics. Two basic worldviews are clashing in our culture, the Judeo-Christian view and the secular humanist view. In other words, it essentially boils down to a confrontation between a theistic view of man and an atheistic view.

Dr. James Hitchcock, a professor of European history at St. Louis University laid out the nature of the conflict between the Judeo-Christian worldview and the secular humanist worldview in an essay entitled *Competing Ethical Systems*. Hitchcock's article is one of the clearest explanations of the ethical clash I have ever read. In it, he notes that we live in a time of pluralism, where competing moral views are vying for power and influence in society. He accurately observes, however, that a society cannot remain permanently fragmented with respect to values.[1]

He also observes that the call for tolerance is a request that the reigning orthodoxy make way for newer points of view. But in practice, the proponents of the new point of view have no intention of tolerating what was once orthodox. Once in the ascendancy, the new worldview will suppress the old. This is occurring in our nation between Judeo-Christian morality and the relativistic, materialistic worldview of secular humanism. With humanism on the rise, the Christian viewpoint is being marginalized and actually suppressed in many areas of our culture. This suppression of the Judeo-Christian worldview is nowhere more evident than in our public schools, where secularism has become the official state religion.

The secularization of the medical profession, and especially the field of bioethics, leads to the dehumanization and devaluing of human life. The secular bioethicist does not accord validity to the intrinsic value of individuals; he views humans as simply clever animals without ultimate meaning or value.

The secular bioethicist bases his worldview on *Humanist Manifestos I* and *II*, as well as the writings of such philosophers as John Stuart Mill. Mill's utilitarian philosophy has seriously compromised the integrity of the medical profession by reducing life and death decisions to questions of utility and autonomous choice. The morality of the behavior itself is not considered, only the free and uncoerced decision by the autonomous individual. The guiding ethical principle of most of our physicians and bioethicists is the idea of maximizing individual freedom (autonomy). Unhindered freedom is the goal, as long as that freedom doesn't harm others and no coercion is involved. Every individual is then free to choose his own values, without necessarily considering how the decisions impact others or the community.

The concept of radical individualism and unlimited individual rights profoundly impacts medical ethics. Once a supposed right is discovered—such as the supposed right to die, proponents rush to defend it. Those who oppose this newly discovered right are seen as rigid, repressive, and clinging to outmoded religious superstitions.

The right to suicide, the right to physician-assisted dying, the right to unrestrained sexual activities—all of these rights are now actively promoted by organizations and individuals who view radical autonomy as the highest good in our society.

It is interesting to me, however, that a number of secular bioethicists are still opposed to a so-called right to suicide or physician-assisted suicide. One reason they are opposing these new rights is to counter the arguments of pro-life doctors and activists who have long predicted the eventual legalization of infanticide, condoned suicide, and euthanasia as a logical consequence of having legalized abortion on demand. The American Medical Association and numerous state-based medical societies are on record as opposing physician-assisted suicide—even while they still support a right of abortion on demand. On the other hand, political activists and the *New England Journal of Medicine* are actively promoting the idea of doctors helping their patients die.

Secular ethicists are not guided by moral absolutes yet continue to assert their personal opinions about life and death issues as fact. In spite of this commitment to moral relativism, they still recognize physicians should not destroy the professional relationship between the doctor and the patient. They want to keep physicians out of the "killing" business in order to sustain the valid role of physician as healer.

With the pro-abortion Clinton administration in power and Hillary Clinton overseeing the reformation of our health care system, it is conceivable that all hospitals (even Catholic hospitals) will soon be legally constrained to provide abortions—and eventually physician aid-in-dying—as a requirement for hospitals receiving federal aid. With economic hard times looming in our country, hospitals will feel the financial strain and euthanasia would help solve some of the fiscal problems facing hospitals and society. Nursing homes will feel the strain even more acutely as they provide long-term care for individuals whose lives may not be considered worth living by cost-controlling administrators and accountants.

We are entering a period of history in this country where physician-assisted suicide threatens to become commonplace, unless there is a concerted effort to reverse the dehumanization of groups such as the chronically ill, the handicapped, the demented, or the comatose patient.

Presently, we have moved beyond the point of simply removing ventilators from those who are dying. The ethicists sustained by the courts have decided that food and hydration constitute medical care, and hospitals now have permission to starve patients to death whose lives are considered burdensome and no longer worth living. At this point, people in nursing homes, the senile, and the chronically ill are at risk of being allowed-to-die by starvation and/or assisted-in-dying. There is only a very short step from starving a person to death to validating a lethal injection to hasten death.

This nation is at a crossroads in dealing with the seminal ethical issues of life and death. We are going to have to decide whether or not we will accept the Jack Kevorkian brand of medical care—or whether we will reject killing as normative and begin seriously developing valid alternatives. We need to develop palliative care programs with improved pain control measures and hospice care with support services for families who are dealing with the chronically or terminally ill or disabled.

We must choose the Judeo-Christian worldview over the secularist viewpoint in responding to the handicapped, the chronically ill, or the dying. Ultimately, what this whole issue boils down to is a clash between those who believe in the transcendent meaning and purpose of human life, and those who deny spirituality, life after death, and judgment.

If there is no God, no ultimate meaning in life, no life after death, and no punishments or rewards after death, then the secularist viewpoint is quite rational. Even so, it is an inadequate worldview and ethic that inevitably leads to the dehumanization and the devaluing of human life—and ultimately results in killing and a return to pagan shamanism where the doctor takes on the role of a witch doctor with powers to kill as well as to heal. As Nigel Cameron has noted in *The New Medicine*,

> The new medicine is the medicine of the new paganism, seeking once more to turn the physician into someone who can kill as well as cure, who has the power over the lives of his patients, to heal and to destroy. . . . Killing has been restored to clinical practice and the clock put back to the days before Hippocrates.[2]

The Judeo-Christian viewpoint, however, places a high value on human life, created in God's image. This view of life and of mankind is enriching and results in a truly compassionate response to the suffering of others. The Christian goal in medicine is to heal, to relieve suffering, and to provide the patient emotional and spiritual comfort while going through the dying process. If the patient is severely ill or handicapped, the goal is to treat the person with respect and love and provide for his basic needs. It is not truly compassionate to suggest that we abandon and kill those who are an inconvenience to us. It is cruel and inhumane and debases us as a civilized society with ordered liberty.

How Bioethicists do Conduct Ethics

The two worldviews competing in the medical field are diametrically opposed. The secular ethicist would do ethics with a totally contrasting set of presuppositions than the Christian ethicist.

The secularist would begin with a number of assumptions:

1. There is no God;
2. Ethics is situational and relative;
3. Ethics is self-actualizing and self-fulfilling, needing no outside justification;
4. An autonomous right to choose makes it always right for him;
5. Human life has relative, rather than absolute value;
6. Life has no ultimate meaning or purpose.

The Christian, on the other hand, would begin with these presuppositions:

1. God exists;
2. God created man in his image and likeness, and he has eternal value, regardless of his physical or mental condition;
3. Ethics and morality derived from the biblical revelation are objective values for all times, places, and people;
4. Human life is sacred, to be protected and nourished;
5. God has a plan for each of us.

These presuppositions guide the secularist and the orthodox Jew and Christian in their respective pursuits of answers to ethical questions.

The secularist assumes that his purpose is to maximize the freedom of the individual, including killing himself if he wishes, while the Christian is concerned about the needs of the patient including the spirituality of the person. The Christian will attempt to benefit the life of the person who is contemplating suicide, rather than to assist him in killing himself.

The secularist is primarily concerned about the autonomous self and the self's desires; the Christian ethicist is concerned about the self as well, but in the larger context, he is concerned about how others will be affected by the actions of the individual. The Christian believes that an individual is to be autonomous, but that in order to maximize freedom for all, individual choices must be made in the context of ordered liberty and responsibility to others. The individual has rights, of course, but those rights are limited by a concern for others. The individual acts in the social context of the community, balancing rights with responsibilities. The right to free speech, for example, does not mean that a person has the unrestricted right to yell "FIRE!" in a crowded theater. Individual rights must always be balanced against the rights of others in a civilized society.

An individual has responsibilities within a society to those around him. In dealing with bioethical dilemmas, we must challenge the idea that individuals have the right to kill themselves or have someone else kill them. There is not, and cannot be, an unrestricted right to die.

Theistic Ethics Versus Secularist Ethics

The classical definition of ethics defines it as the science of moral duty, of ideal human character and the ideal ends of human action. It deals with moral philosophy and is concerned with both conduct and character. It is also concerned with how we can discern the differences between right and wrong, good and evil in the ethical decision-making process.

Regrettably, this classic view of ethics has fallen into disfavor by the secular relativists. When they deal with ethical issues, they dwell on radical individualism and an amoral approach, rather than on concepts of good or bad, right or wrong ideals of behavior. In the humanist worldview, ethical conduct becomes whatever a person chooses for himself unless it causes harm to others or is coerced.

Modern ethics, then, depends upon the individual's over-arching worldview—the religious and/or philosophical tenets, principles, or presuppositions. As such, ethics is inevitably expressed as behavior (morality) within the social context, whether it addresses medicine, law, or sexuality. Ethics is derived from one's worldview and is expressed as behavior, the morality of the culture. Morality is behavior, what a person does. Bioethicists engaged in discourse about a particular ethical dilemma focus their attention on the particular case at hand yet are guided by their view of the nature of man—whether moral man or amoral man.

To clearly understand the significance of one's worldview and how it determines ethics and ultimately influences behavior in a society, let's compare the elements of the two worldviews in conflict:

1. **God**: The Christian worldview sees God as the creator and sustainer of all. God provides the *truth* by which individuals and society must abide.

The secular humanist denies the existence of God or declares Him to be irrelevant. There is no absolute truth.

2. **Eternity**: The Christian sees the long-term (eternal) view of human life.

The secularist has a short-term view of man and of human life. He denies or is skeptical about eternity.

3. **Values**: The Christian believes in absolute values. What we do right now has an objective value and because of this, life has ultimate, moral significance.

The secularist believes values are situational. What we choose to do autonomously in the now is all that matters. There are no moral absolutes; everything is relative, dependent on the situation where individual choice is all important.

4. **Purpose**: The Christian believes we are here to glorify God and enjoy Him forever. We are to love God and practice self-control and selflessness in our relationships with others.

The secularist worships the self. The ultimate purpose in life is self-actualization and self-fulfillment. Relationships are conditional upon meeting one's own desires (hedonism).

5. **Toleration**: Christians are called to be tolerant, but not of ideas or activities that violate God's Word.

The secularist is willing to tolerate any behavior as long as it is freely chosen, does not harm others, and is void of coercion. The secularist, however, is extremely intolerant of those who appear intolerant by endorsing positive values such as duty and obligation.

6. **Freedom**: The Judeo-Christian believes in the responsible exercise of freedom accountable to the laws of God. There is no absolute freedom or license, but limited freedom with responsibility to others and to the community.

The secularist believes in liberation as license with minimal external or internal constraints allowed—the minimalist ethic. While the secularist viewpoint is considered liberating to the individual, it is in fact inadequate to sustain a valid culture or society.

As Heritage Foundation scholar William Donohue has noted in *The New Freedom*,

> If enough people in any society refuse, for whatever reason, to act in a civil manner toward their fellow man, order descends to anarchy and society is harmed, perhaps irreparably. Society is based on rules, on norms that must be observed. Without standards of right and wrong, each person does as he pleases, following the dictates of his interests and passions. Civility ceases to exist and chaos reigns. Freedom is ruled out for everyone.[3]

As Donohue notes, an irresponsible devotion to radical autonomy—freedom as license—leads to social destruction and chaos. And this destruction has taken root in the ethics of medical practice, where the secular humanist worldview has gained ascendancy.

The secularist worldview, although it ostensibly brings freedom, actually brings social decay and death. It is an inadequate ethic to sustain a civil order.

We desperately need to return not only to the Judeo-Christian worldview in medical ethical decision-making, but physicians should return to the sound, life-affirming ethical principles expressed in the secular Hippocratic Oath as truth affirmed by history.

Discarding the Hippocratic Tradition

The secularists who currently dominate ethical thinking in the medical profession not only have rejected the Judeo-Christian worldview which was the basis for western civilization; they have also rejected the Hippocratic tradition, which was based on pagan Greek polytheistic thinking.

The Hippocratic tradition in medicine, although pagan in origin, presaged the Judeo-Christian tradition and provided an ethical foundation that was respected by the medical profession for over 1,900 years. It provided an ethical framework which rejected pagan shamanism and called physicians to a higher standard of behavior as healers, not killers. It provided physicians with a limit to behaviors that could be destructive of the doctor/patient relationship. In this oath, it established a trust relationship between the doctor and patient that served medicine well for centuries before it was discarded as outmoded.

Dangerous Ideas

The newer secularist ideas in medicine have undermined the paternalistic role of the physician in providing care to his patient. This has been replaced by the ideas of patient autonomy and the quality-of-life ethic.

The idea of patient autonomy lies in contrast to the traditional paternalistic role of the physician. Up until about fifteen years ago, the physician had a somewhat fatherly role in providing medical care for his patients. He/she assumed an advocacy role for his patient and was expected to personally act in the best interest of his patient. This paternalistic role was part of the Hippocratic tradition of trust and responsibility.

Patient autonomy and self-determination have placed the paternalistic role of the doctor in major medical decision-making in the hands of the patient or his surrogate. This has been beneficial to patient rights though it has diminished the primary advocacy role of the physician to act in the patient's best interest. The patient, and often his family members, may not necessarily be equipped to make appropriate medical decisions. Very often a patient will enter the hospital with painful injury or illness and be so distraught that he will beg to be put out of his misery. Should the physician listen to him and provide him with a lethal injection? Or should he use his medical knowledge to provide pain control measures and start the healing process through medicine or surgery? If the doctor is truly an advocate for a patient, he will not even consider killing the patient as a form of medical service.

The concept of patient autonomy has been ultimately expressed with the passage of the previously mentioned Patient Self-Determination Act of 1990 by the U.S. Congress. Although I am sure this is well-intentioned legislation, the act has driven a wider wedge between the physician and the patient. Under this law, any person entering a hospital which receives federal funds must sign a form which requires him to give an advance directive on how he should be treated should he become incapacitated while hospitalized.

This effectively bypasses the physician, family members, the bioethics committee, etc., placing the control of medical decisions in the hands of a fearful and an often uninformed patient. This application of the patient autonomy principle actually may forfeit authority to third parties to make patient care decisions. As a result, economic factors enter. The need to control costs enters into the treatment/non-treatment decision. When economic considerations for the institution and/or the family burden such decisions, it takes little imagination to see how aid-in-dying might be adopted as a cost-saving measure.

The advance directive, though well-intended, has often complicated the relationship between the patient and doctor and limited the doctor's options in advocating for the patient. In particular, emergency situations render the advanced directive dysfunctional. With multiple health professionals working on someone who may have been rushed to the hospital with a heart attack, no one is going to have the availability or the time to check the patient's medical records for any advanced directives.

In non-emergency situations, the advanced directive may impede the thoughtful physician from exercising his clinical discernment and knowledge in providing the best treatment for his patient.

In brief, rejection of paternalism in favor of patient-directed medical decisions does not necessarily assure the execution of actions in the best interests of the patient or family members. It places the patient and family at risk by interfering with the ideal of a trusting relationship between the patient, physician, and family members.

The quality-of-life ethic is clearly subjective and remarkably variable. The secularist rejects the idea that all human life is sacred, having ultimate meaning and significance. In rejecting a sanctity of life ethic, secularists logically can accept killing—aid-in-dying—as a means of solving personal, social, and economic problems.

Those who are in need of medical care would do well to realize that each hospital or medical facility is governed by an over-arching philosophy. That philosophy will govern how medical care is provided in that particular facility. It will either adhere to a quality-of-life ethic, the sanctity of life ethic, or a blending of the two. A Catholic institution will usually be committed to the sanctity of life ethic and will instruct its physicians to err on the side of life when making medical decisions; a public hospital or institution will most likely have a secular quality-of-life ethic, placing a relative value on human lives.

In seeking medical care, it would be important for individuals with a commitment to a pro-life position to ascertain the philosophical leanings of the doctors and hospitals they visit.

The Loss of Personal Care

As modern physicians have ignored or rejected the Hippocratic Oath, we have seen a de-personalization take place in the doctor/patient relationship. A number of factors are responsible for this unfortunate development. Doctors who consider themselves technicians instead of healers have brought about a decline in the trust relationship with their patients.

Another factor that I have found regrettable is the interference of third party payers in the physician/patient relationship. I attempted to halt the acceptance of insurance company payments directly to physicians back in the mid-1960s because it would interfere with the close, professional, personal relationship that should exist between the patient and the doctor. The American Medical Association led a short and unsuccessful fight opposing direct third-party reimbursements in order to avoid this interference and to maintain the professional relationship between patient and doctor.

When the insurance companies would pay claims directly to the patients, who would then pay the physician, it was understood, as part of your professional code of ethics, that though you might not get paid, your patient care would not be dependent on a third party's agreement.

When I first entered my practice in the late 1950s, I can remember not getting more than four or five hours sleep each night for the first three years because of a personal obligation to treat the indigent and needy patients. Night after night physicians took care of the sick—without compensation—as this was expected of a medical professional in those days.

Unfortunately, we have lost that personal relationship with the welcome advances in technology, the interference of third party payers, and the increasing subspecialization that has taken place in the profession.

Filling the Ethical Vacuum

When all is said and done, our medical profession is facing a spiritual crisis that can only be aided by adhering to a Judeo-Christian worldview. As part of the first step to restoring our profession to its once-noble calling as the healing arts, our physicians should declare their adherence to the Hippocratic Oath.

As a second and more important step, Christian physicians should become more active than they have been in medical societies, in bioethical think tanks and in our legislatures to promote the Judeo-Christian viewpoint on the sanctity of life—as opposed to the quality of life ethic.

A third step would be for Christian physicians to seriously consider a principled persuasion of non-Christian associates in the profession.

We *must*, as a profession, return to our roots of the Hippocratic and Judeo-Christian tradition or we will continue to go the way of the Nazi doctors. We *cannot* allow our profession to become paganized by secular humanist thinking. We *cannot* be both healers and killers and still call ourselves civilized.

Chapter 10

Doctors: Licensed to Kill

In his article, "Medical Science Under Dictatorship," Dr. Leo Alexander analyzed the ethical changes which took place in the German medical community in the early 1920s. Alexander noted that the philosophical justification for killing the handicapped, the mentally retarded, and eventually all non-Germans began with an article by Dr. Karl Binding and Professor Dr. Alfred Hoche, M.D. entitled "Releasing Persons from Lives Devoid of Value." This essay has recently been reprinted by the National Legal Center for the Medically Dependent and Disabled as "Permitting the Destruction of Unworthy Life."[1]

Alexander observed that German physicians as well as psychiatrists readily accepted this new relativistic view of life. This change in the way human life was valued set the stage for Hitler's Holocaust and the murder of an estimated six million Jews and four million non-Jews, including Russians, gypsies, Poles, and others who were considered a threat to German racial purity.

Alexander also notes that during the Nazi occupation of The Netherlands, the Dutch physicians successfully resisted the temptation to adopt the Nazi doctor's philosophy of compassionate killing. According to Alexander, "It is to the everlasting honor of the medical profession of Holland that they recognized the earliest and most subtle phases of this attempt and rejected it."[2]

When the Nazis issued a decree that the Dutch physicians engage in mass killings of the unwanted, they turned in their medical licenses as a protest. The Nazis then arrested one hundred physicians and sent them off to concentration camps. The remaining physicians, however, stood strong and still resisted. As a result of their solidarity, not a single euthanasia or sterilization case was performed by any Dutch physician during the Nazi occupation.

The Sad State of Dutch Medicine Today

Regrettably, the bravery of the Dutch physicians under the Nazi occupation has given way to an eager acceptance of euthanasia—even involuntary euthanasia—in modern Holland. In fact, the Dutch physicians are considered *leaders* in adopting policies which allow physicians to kill their patients. In early 1993, after more than twenty years of tacit acceptance of physician-assisted killing, the Dutch parliament, by a vote of 91-45, established guidelines which effectively legalize the "compassionate killing" of patients.

The history of the way in which this occurred in Holland is instructive—and should serve as a clear warning to those who deny the slippery slope. One of the most detailed accounts describing the Dutch acceptance and practice of *medicide* is found in an essay by Dr. Richard Fenigsen, formerly a cardiologist at Willem-Alexander Hospital, s-Hertogenbosch, The Netherlands.

Writing on "Euthanasia in the Netherlands," published in *Issues in Law and Medicine*, Fenigsen observes that the current acceptance of euthanasia in Holland gained a foothold in the minds of physicians in 1969 with the publication of Dr. Jan Hendrik van den Berg's book, *Medical Power and Medical Ethics*.[3]

Van den Berg, a professor of neurology, stated that it was time for physicians to reject the idea of an unconditional right to life because of advances in technology and what he called medical power. It was time, he said, to exercise this new medical power by freeing physicians to terminate life. Van den Berg's book became an instant best seller, going through ten printings in the first year of publication and twenty-five printings in all.

Van den Berg promoted the idea that defective children should not be allowed to live. It was his belief that doctors have a duty to terminate those whose lives were meaningless. He openly recommended involuntary euthanasia as a way of dealing with those whose lives were considered not worthy to be lived.

According to Dr. Fenisgen, Van den Berg's suggestions were eagerly accepted by both Protestant and Catholic ministers, intellectuals, and bioethical think tanks. His promotion of involuntary euthanasia became so well accepted by the Dutch that a poll taken in 1986 indicated that 77 percent of the public supported the concept.[4]

In 1985, the Royal Dutch Society of Medicine declared its support for the involuntary compassionate killing of handicapped newborn babies, minors, mentally retarded, the demented, and in cases where the patient cannot express himself but where it is assumed he or she would want to be killed. In 1988, Dutch medical journals published reports of the denial of lifesaving surgery to Downs syndrome babies including moral justifications. According to Fenisgen, an estimated three hundred handicapped babies are allowed to die in Holland each year and at least ten are actively killed by physicians. He notes that those physicians who write in justification of killing handicapped children are deliberate in their efforts to dehumanize these children. They describe handicapped children in such terms as severely misshapen, incomplete, unfit, or heavily disfigured. Fenisgen observes, "Those babies are not viewed as *people* with a disability or disease; it is their whole being that is devalued, their humanity represented as incomplete and questioned."[5]

The pro-euthanasia physicians argue that to treat a handicapped baby is an insolent display of medical power, a meaningless action, and a violation of the patient's privacy and bodily integrity—and, amazingly enough—a premeditated, severe bodily injury punishable under Article 300 of the Dutch Penal Code.[6] In the minds of these pro-death doctors, it is a *crime* to attempt to heal a handicapped child.

This philosophy is clearly shown in the writings of J.C. Molenaar, a leading Dutch pediatric surgeon; K. Gill, a professor of family medicine; and Dupuis, a medical ethicist. These men argue against lifesaving help to children with Downs syndrome because the value of a life depends on how valuable the life is for *other people*. In their thinking, no one has an inherent right to life. A person is valuable only if other people think he is. If no one values a handicapped child, the child should be exterminated.

Involuntary Euthanasia Widely Practiced

In a study conducted in 1989 by the Mediolegal Group at Limburg University in Maastricht, 299 doctors were asked if they had performed euthanasia without a patient's request. One hundred and twenty-three doctors (41.1 percent) answered *yes*. Eighty-eight doctors had performed involuntary euthanasia from one to four times; twenty-four doctors had killed from five to ten people; four doctors had killed from eleven to fifteen people; and seven doctors had killed more than fifteen each.[7]

In a report by the Dutch government on the extent of euthanasia in Holland, it was revealed that in 1990 there were 2,300 cases of voluntary euthanasia, 400 assisted suicides, and more than 1,000 cases of euthanasia without a request from the patient. Doctors also helped hasten the deaths of 16,850 others—8,750 by withholding or withdrawing treatment and 8,100 by providing pain-killing drugs to hasten death.

In all of the 8,750 cases and in 5,000 of the 8,100 cases, the patient had not consented to this treatment. In short, Dutch physicians in 1990 admitted that they sought to kill twenty thousand patients—almost all without the permission of the patient. In addition, 70 percent of euthanasia cases are dishonestly certified by doctors as natural deaths.[8]

Holland: A Glimpse of the Future in the U.S.

Unless our medical ethic changes in the U.S., we can expect to follow the trend toward euthanasia as practiced in Holland. As we look back over the past twenty to twenty-five years, there has been a change in our culture from a basic Judeo-Christian ethos and ethic to the prevailing secular humanist ethos and ethic. We have progressively moved from a sanctity of life ethic to a quality-of-life ethic. As a result of this shift in our worldview, we have created a culture which now accepts the killing of the unborn child, for any reason or for no reason at all, as a woman's absolute, individual right to choose. We have faced and blunted the humanistic agenda for infanticide and the limiting of the lives of those who are handicapped. We are now moving on to the consideration of condoned suicide and the right to die. This trend is accelerated by the missions of Derek Humphry and Jack Kevorkian who support physician-assisted suicide and the eventual acceptance of active voluntary and involuntary euthanasia.

The Dutch experience should shock us into a realization that the same pro-death philosophy that pervades the Dutch medical profession has infiltrated our medical profession as well. One of the most frightening aspects of the Dutch euthanasia movement is called *crypthanasia*, which involves the clandestine killing of patients. A typical example of crypthanasia might involve an older man who has suffered a heart attack and is being treated in an emergency room. His condition is treatable with a pacemaker, but because of his age and the cost of care, he is denied appropriate treatment and is allowed to die—or even assisted in dying (killed)—by a physician who decides he is not worth saving. This is done without the patient's or his family's knowledge or consent. This practice of involuntary euthanasia represents a homicide or murder—yet this is acceptable non-treatment by Dutch physicians and is considered routine medical practice.

The practice of crypthanasia may have been an unforeseen development among those who advocate euthanasia, but the fact is that this represents a clear example of how a quality-of-life ethic leads ultimately to the "compassionate killing" of patients.

This requires new considerations as we wrestle with the euthanasia issue. Where do we draw the line between a right to die and a duty to die? This question will inevitably impact the elderly, those who are feeble and who may feel they are a burden to their children or to society. Once we accept the notion that there is a right to die it doesn't take much rationalizing to accept the idea that there may also be a duty to die and that our medical profession has an obligation to help people along in the dying process—even against their will.

Once people become accustomed to the idea that personal, social, and economic problems can be solved by killing, it is very likely that suicide clinics will become as commonplace as abortion clinics. Once compassionate killing becomes acceptable medical practice, this would, in effect, be the end of modern medicine as we have known it.

If physician-assisted killing becomes normative, we will have returned to barbarianism, and our profession will have returned to the ethic and medical practice preceding the Hippocratic Oath—a giant step backward of over two thousand years.

We should recapture our history and our ethics which were based primarily on the Hippocratic Oath blended with Judeo-Christian morality. The Greeks, with their polytheistic culture, had the wisdom to realize that the physician could not serve a dual role as healer and killer if he was to truly benefit those in his care. The Hippocratic Oath clearly proscribed abortion, infanticide, assisted suicide, and euthanasia and gave the physician clear direction as to his professional conduct as teacher and advocate for his patients.

The Hippocratic tradition served as the basis for western medicine for centuries and enabled the physician to maintain an honorable and essential professional relationship with his patient. We simply cannot allow the compassionate killers to continue leading the medical profession down the slippery slope by accepting the killing of patients as a medical service.

A truly frightening aspect of the pro-death movement is that we have forgotten the history of what happened in Nazi Germany and what is currently occurring in Holland. We should have learned that there are limits as to how far men can go in solving personal, social, economic, and political problems by killing. Certainly, in Western civilization we are facing many of the same problems which captured the attention of the pre-Nazi and Nazi era doctors. What we must resist is the temptation to dehumanize groups of individuals whose lives are considered "not worthy to be lived."

We must remember that the first step in the killing process begins with the dehumanizing of those groups targeted for death. Those groups most likely to be dehumanized are the physically handicapped, the mentally retarded, the demented, and other so-called non-productive citizens regarded as useless eaters. The risks are increased remarkably in hard times.

We Must Draw the Line

We must learn from history and refuse to accept current proposals which would legalize the killing of individuals and groups of individuals perceived as burdensome. There are valid and truly compassionate alternatives to killing.

First of all, those who are ill or handicapped need to have access to health care and adequate rehabilitative services. A national priority should be to make certain that people who are disabled or chronically ill have access to adequate medical treatment.

Secondly, we must recognize that one of the greatest

fears facing someone who is handicapped, ill, or dying is the issue of pain. We must make it a priority in our medical training institutions that medical personnel be prepared to provide palliative care—adequate pain relief. There is adequate knowledge and available means to control pain, alleviate suffering, and assure true dignity in caring, not killing.

Third, our society must respond to the need of those who are terminally ill by supporting the family as well as the dying through appropriate hospice care.

Unfortunately, the Christian community does not seem to have responded very well to the needs of the terminally ill, much as the Christian community failed to provide valid alternatives to abortion. The efforts to deal with the abortion issue in the mid- to late-seventies were inadequate in providing pregnant women access to obstetrical care as well as financial and personal/social support services. The pro-life community, in effect, incriminated itself by responding too slowly in meeting the needs of pregnant women while decrying abortion. In particular, the adoption option was not strongly advocated. The Christian community, in my opinion, is now missing a similar opportunity by not dealing aggressively with the euthanasia issue. The Christian church should be taking a leadership role in providing palliative and hospice care for the chronically and terminally ill.

Fourth, we must resist efforts to allow the acceptance of suicide as a right. There are effective suicide prevention programs in this country. Again, the Christian community should be leading in helping to preserve the lives of those who feel that death is their only option.

History and experience teaches us that suicide is a culturally determined phenomenon. In Japan, for example, suicide was once an accepted choice for those who had lost face. As a result of its acceptance, the suicide rates were high. In ancient Rome, suicide was considered an act of courage, and it flourished.

If we condone suicide as simply a person's right, we

will have more and more people killing themselves. We cannot accept this as a right. We must provide every resource at our disposal to *prevent* individuals from killing themselves. It is not compassionate to accept suicide as a solution to personal and social problems.

Forced Death?

If the compassionate killers are not halted, there may come a time when the medical profession, with the help of the state, will participate in the killing of classes or groups of individuals. I do not believe this is a foolish statement. Based upon history and observing current medical trends in this country, I believe we may see a time when it is considered good medical practice to provide assisted dying (killing) of certain individuals or groups. When economic hardship hits this country, there will be a great temptation to solve skyrocketing health care costs by rationing health care and by eliminating many individuals whose lives are not deemed worth living.

Who would the compassionate killers target for *forced* death? I believe our physicians would follow the same pattern as in pre-Nazi Germany. They would probably target the mentally ill and severely disabled groups first, including those mentally ill homeless who are an economic burden to society.

A second target may be AIDS patients. These are individuals who are suffering from an incurable disease and who die slow and painful deaths. Their hospital care is expensive, and there is no hope of curing them. They would be logical targets of forced death. A third target may be those in nursing homes who are bedridden, chronically ill, or simply senile. A fourth target to be considered would be our prison population. We have doubled the number of prisoners in the last ten years. Our prisons are terribly overcrowded. What better population to kill than prisoners?

Many people naively think that because we have a democratic system, it would never be possible for our medical profession or government to require the death of certain unwanted groups. It is assumed that our constitution would protect the targeted groups from killing. This is wishful thinking. The medical profession and society have already accepted the killing of unborn babies as an ethical practice. The current worldview which pervades the medical profession is accepting more of the idea of physician aid-in-dying and a right to die. There is already a philosophical and ethical foundation in place for the concept of compassionate killing as part of standard medical practice. There is only a short step from a doctor believing there is a right to die to the concept that a person has a duty to die. If a person has a duty to die, it may be the obligation of the physician and state to *require* an individual to die.

The Judeo-Christian World View—
Our Only Hope

As I look back over the history of the medical profession and western civilization, I am convinced that the only ethic or worldview that can preserve the sanctity of life and a truly compassionate, just society is the Judeo-Christian worldview.

Our entire Western civilization was founded upon Judeo-Christian beliefs about life and the derivative fundamental values of liberty and the dignity of the individual in the sight of God. As a result of the influence of these views about man and his relationship to God, we have developed a civilized culture that respects an individual's right to life—regardless of its quality. Anyone taking an honest look at the history of Europe and the United States must admit that the Judeo-Christian worldview was the basis for civilization. This high view of man stimulated social, cultural, political, and economic developments which brought freedom and prosperity to nations. This view still holds great promise for the future of mankind in terms of freedom and the social order.

Christians, out of compassion, founded hospitals, orphanages, schools, and other ministries to meet the needs of those who were ill, uneducated, lonely, poverty-stricken, and mentally ill. They believed in the inherent dignity of men, women, and children who were made in the image and likeness of God. They used their talents to bring hope and healing to those who were suffering. As a result of these efforts, Christians were a civilizing and compassionate influence in society.

Regrettably, however, the secular humanist worldview has invaded our society and has brought moral and social decay, death and chaos with it. We can see the negative influence of materialist thought everywhere around us— in sexual immorality, in crime, in homosexuality, child abuse, divorce, pornography, etc.

In every area of our culture, one can see personal and institutional decay that has occurred as the result of our nation rejecting the Judeo-Christian worldview. We are beset by the results of an inadequate moral and social ethic bringing destruction with it.

The only valid hope for this nation is to return to our Judeo-Christian ethos and ethic as the basis for civil society. If we deny the return to our religious roots, our nation is doomed to cultural warfare which will Balkanize our country. We will become a nation of warring tribes, rather than one nation and one people united by a common moral consensus. If materialism and relativism are not challenged and brought under control, we will progress to authoritarianism, a loss of human freedom, and ultimately into social chaos and endless conflict.

What Needs to be Done?

There are a number of ways that individuals who support Judeo-Christian values can impact the culture and political system. There is no question that a desperate need exists for traditionalists to get involved in the political system to elect people who share their views. There must be an aggressive effort on the part of Christians and others who share Judeo-Christian values to contend for the faith in the public square. Secularism must be rejected, and the importance of belief in our transcendent spiritual and objective moral being is necessary for the survival of our system of government. This must be emphasized in the public debate.

One of our primary efforts should be to develop and maintain crisis pregnancy centers. We must assure that pregnant women have access to support services and medical care. We should continue to stigmatize the abortionist so that abortion becomes less available as an option. I believe that the abortion issue may eventually be solved at the local level by educational efforts aimed at making abortion less acceptable and available.

We must maintain protective laws for our children and resist the so-called children's rights movement which would abrogate parental authority and place power in the hands of social engineers and government.

We must insist on maintaining clear social and legal sanctions against the idea of a right to suicide. We should provide laws that prohibit the right to suicide or the supposed right of a physician to assist someone in killing himself—as Michigan recently did to deal with Jack Kevorkian. In addition, we should provide prevention, intervention, and support services to diminish the incidence of suicide in our society.

We must reassert the value of human life, respect, and true dignity for the dying in caring and comfort. We should reject the idea of active euthanasia and pass laws prohibiting physicians or other medical personnel from providing compassionate killing as a solution to personal, social, and economic problems.

We must be committed to providing care for AIDS patients and should resist efforts by the compassionate killers to target AIDS patients for killing. Regrettably, with the burden of HIV/AIDS, the medical profession and others will be called upon to practice active voluntary euthanasia on these patients. It occurs quietly, but we should never allow this practice to become legalized.

Impacting the Bioethical Debate

Those who would like to impact the debate on bioethical issues must first become informed on the issues involved. They must realize that these issues will eventually involve them, their family, and those around them. They must get involved in organizations that support traditional values and that are fighting to restore Judeo-Christian morality and a respect-for-life ethic as the basis of bioethical thinking.

In gaining an understanding of the life and death issues involved, individuals must become active in presenting their views in the public square. They must express themselves forcefully (without abusive language or intimidation) with well-honed arguments appropriate for both a secular and theistic audience. They should present these views at meetings of the school board, county commissioner, city council, health agencies, as well as in the press and in their church.

What about physicians? There are still a significant number who hold to traditional beliefs. These individuals should be encouraged to join in making an impact for traditional values in their professional contacts and medical associations. They should be encouraged to consciously commit themselves to bearing witness to the truth which is revealed in history and in biblical revelation as to the sanctity of life and the vital pragmatic importance of the Judeo-Christian worldview.

Pro-life and pro-family physicians should realize the moral influence they can have within their communities. They should realize, as C.S. Lewis pointed out, that each of us is a moral being. He observed that with the loss of Christian values, we would see the abolition of man and of civilization. Physicians who accept this truth must commit themselves to act as moral beings in their communities and stand up for Judeo-Christian morality as the *only* way to prevent the destruction of our civilization as we have known it.

Conclusion

If we do not halt the efforts of the compassionate killers, our nation faces a frighteningly violent and death-filled future. The secular humanist ethic dominant in our culture will inevitably lead to social chaos and destruction because it is based on a faulty view of the nature of man, the nature of God, and man's relationship with God and his fellow man. A false premise will ultimately lead to faulty conclusions, not only in bioethical issues, but in all issues of human life and human relationships. The secular humanist ideology and its commitment to radical autonomy and moral relativism is a failed system and cannot sustain a valid civilized culture. If allowed to progress, this faulty ethical system will bring cultural collapse and anarchy to our society.

It is absolutely essential for the survival of this nation that we actively, consistently, and aggressively oppose materialism/relativism, its inadequate ethic, and its dehumanizing, pro-death philosophy.

On the other hand, we must promote the God-given truths embodied in the Judeo-Christian worldview. It is this worldview that will protect the value of human life; that will foster stable families; that will encourage morality and sustain ordered liberty and civilized behavior in a truly humane society.

Appendix A

When Does Life Begin?

In 1984, I sponsored a pro-life seminar in Pensacola and gave this speech to explain what the current scientific literature was saying about when human life begins.

Dialogue on the subject of abortion has been next to impossible. Certainly to a large extent this is due to the emotional nature of the issue. But, it is also due in significant part to the misinformation and confusion over the particular question: When does human life begin?

Surprisingly, there is fundamental agreement on this subject among honest and informed advocates on both sides of the abortion question. I would hope to provide an answer—a scientific answer—to the question of the beginning of human life so that dialogue can proceed with the value question, *viz.*, granted that abortion kills human life, when, if ever, can this killing be justified?

WHEN DOES LIFE BEGIN? is one of the most crucial questions in the critical life issue of abortion. Advocates of women's abortion rights and advocates of the unborn's rights answer this question differently, but they agree that the question is key.

Responses one gets to this question are many and varied: Life begins at conception (fertilization); nidation, implantation (7-10 days); onset of the heartbeat (4 weeks); onset of brain function (7-8 weeks); fetal movement, quickening (4 months); viability (surviving outside of the womb); birth; social interaction; consciousness of self (8-10 months); age of reason; and often simply—it is a question science cannot answer and it is just a matter of religion. It so happens that none of these answers are correct. So let's re-examine the question of life. Biology is the science of life. The expert on the subject of life is the biologist. In fact, biological science not only has an answer of when life begins, it has *the answer*.

The biologic/scientific answer is based on fact rather than opinion. Because of this, the scientific answer is objective and not based on bias, prejudice, theologic belief, or philosophic theory. Therefore, the scientific answer is uniquely suited for achieving a consensus. Scientists who strongly oppose abortion commonly agree with scientists who strongly favor abortion in answering the question.

First of all, *what is life*? What kind of life are we talking about? *Webster's Dictionary* gives twenty-one definitions of life. Depending on which definition one chooses, the answer could vary from life existing from all eternity to life beginning at death.

The kind of life that is involved in the abortion issue is biological life. This kind of life is free of subjective interpretation and therefore suitable for decision-making.

Although the fundamental understanding of biological systems has existed since the mid-1980s, there is no generally accepted definition of biological life because there is disagreement pertaining to borderline forms of life such as viruses, or, virus-like agents. Fortunately, this does not affect the discussion of life as it pertains to abortion because there is no scientific disagreement about what stage of reproduction is alive and what is not.

So, we might well re-phrase our original question as follows: *In human reproduction, there is a point in time when life begins. When does that point occur?* This question is also faulty, however, because it contains an unwarranted presumption regarding human reproduction, i.e., biological life does not begin; it is continuous.

There is no period when life stops and later starts up again. Cells come only from living cells. If the ovum were not alive and mature, it would never be fertilized. If the sperm were not alive it could never reach the ovum, much less fertilize it. The continuity of life is a principle that scientists agree upon. If life had a beginning at all, it was an event that occurred several thousands of years ago—the origin of life. The important matter is that there is no point or interval from fertilization to birth when the unborn progeny is not alive. Thus, the unborn is at all times alive—it is life.

But, just a minute now. We have included sperm and ovum in the life continuum and thereby blurred the distinction between the germ cells, i.e., the sperm and ovum, and, the zygote or fertilized ovum. We have established that the unborn offspring is at all times alive but *when does life become human?*

The adjective *human* is used to describe that which is characteristic of man as a species distinguished from other animals. Biologically, there are two criteria for what is human: 1) extrinsic criteria and 2) intrinsic criteria. Extrinsically, that which is of human origin is human. By this criteria human applies to sounds, footprints, excrement, etc., as well as human beings.

Intrinsically, being *human* depends upon genetic constitution, and this is the proper criteria for the discussion of abortion. Normally, this constitution is contained in a set of forty-six chromosomes which is present in all the cells of the body except for the germ cells or gametes with twenty-three chromosomes. Thus, the answer to the question: *when does life become human?* is *never*. Just as life is continuous, humanity or humanness is continuous. Intrinsically and extrinsically, the sperm, the ovum, the zygote, and all cells, tissues, and stages that arise from the zygote are human. None of them can ever be characterized as belonging to any other species. Human life is not started, it is transmitted. There is no instance or interval of time between fertilization and birth when the unborn offspring is anything but human.

G.L. Flanagan has noted: "From their first hour, the human cells are distinctly human." Now, however, if life is continuous and humanity or humanness is continuous, what is the difference between the sperm and the ovum before fertilization and the zygote after fertilization? They are all human life, are they not?

There are several crucial differences, however, between a zygote, the conceptus or fertilized ovum, and a sperm or an ovum. The crucial difference is the information content. The sperm and/or ovum have only half of the genetic information that the zygote has, but that alone does not indicate a difference between the zygote and a sperm and an ovum taken together and used in a quantitative sense, i.e., the whole is equal to the sum of the parts. However, in the qualitative sense, the whole i.e., the zygote, is greater than the sum of its parts, i.e., a sperm and an ovum. [*At this point in my speech, I showed a film which depicted the beginning of an individual life.*]

To recap our previous review, the points were established that life is a continuum and humanity or humanness of that life is a continuum. And, as the film illustrated, a totally unique event occurs at conception.

The film relates the biological fact that human beings call other entirely human beings into existence through the material link occurring at conception or fertilization that relates parents to children. We all know that a sperm and ovum, each with its own set of chromosomes, combine to determine the kind of bodily life with which each of us will live in this world. We know that, because each of our parents provided only part of those chromosomes, we are not totally like either of them. Nor are we like any other human being, because the path on which our inherited genes has sent us all is at least a little bit different from any other human being that has ever lived or that will ever exist. All this is common knowledge, i.e., life is transmitted and is transmitted as information via the genetic code. No individual electron, atom, or molecule is transmitted into the next generation—the information is transmitted, not the matter itself.

When Does Life Begin?

What may not be so commonly known, however, is that the newly formed human embryo is, from its very first days, preparing itself to be a parent of another human embryo years later. It will produce another human being who, though equal in its basic human worth, will be an entirely distinct individual from its parents. We all know, it is true, that a new and healthily formed human being is marked as male or female from the day that an X or Y chromosome of the sperm combines with the X chromosome of the ovum. We know, too, that if this combination of sex determining chromosomes is fostered by the right environment in the womb, the appropriate reproduction system of the female or male child will begin to develop visibly—within eight weeks after conception. Thus, the newly forming body is propelled towards one day being able to produce its own offspring.

Also, many of us do not know that the cells which eventually become sperm or ovum do not wait even those eight weeks to appear. Within four days of conception, the hardly more than microscopic embryo has succeeded in producing certain cells that will eventually become sperm or ovum, the germ cells. These highly specialized cells, called gametes, differ from all the cells with which the embryo is forming its own bones, tissues, and organs. These germ cells are structures to become the bones, tissues, and organs of another embryo which will not be conceived until perhaps twenty to thirty years later. Thus, along with the building up of its own structure, one of the first things a new embryo does is to provide cells for the future existence of another entirely distinct human being.

Years later, when the developing embryo is fully maturing, the germ cells will undergo a final development into the completed sperm or ovum. As the final development takes place, the ovum is extremely active within itself, producing certain acids (RNA-Ribonucleic acid) in the extraordinary quantities necessary to support a new embryo, should the ovum be fertilized. Then, suddenly when the ovum reaches maturity, this and other rather exuberant activity inside the ovum comes to a complete halt. In other words, it comes to a halt precisely when the ovum has enough of what it needs to support the beginnings of life of another new human individual. Just as the ovum undergoes these dramatic changes, so also does the sperm cell, but only when it is released into the female genital organs and has managed to get quite close to the ovum. At this point, the front two-thirds of the head of the sperm is softened (capacitation) as an outer layer is dissolved, making it possible for the sperm to penetrate the ovum.

With this penetration, the ovum, sleeping since it reached its optimal quota of RNA and the other chemicals it needs to support a new life, suddenly wakes up and begins to produce extraordinary quantities of protein. According to world-renowned researcher Dr. Jerome LeJeune, the ovum sits like a tape recorder, and when triggered by the sperm, the human symphony starts.

The ovum also toughens its outer surface and makes other changes to prevent another sperm cell from entering. Just as the embryo produced germ cells in its first days of existence so now the mature body which developed from that embryo propels itself toward producing a new human individual. It will be an individual with a combination of chromosomes never seen before and with resulting characteristics unique to itself alone.

As the cells of the new embryo divide into new cells over the first few days, they trigger in one another a process by which they become cells different from one another, i.e., one group takes off on its own to develop nerve tissue; another heart tissue; another bone cells, etc. This process of cells becoming different from one another is stimulated by chemicals in the mother's system, and cannot, once begun, be reversed.

Let us think upon these things. We have reviewed the means by which a new human being—as an embryo a few days old, and as a developing fetus—and finally, as a mature adult—provides the germ cells—precisely these germ cells which, many years later as sperm and ovum, are necessary for the beginning of yet another human being. These are biological facts assessable to the probing of material senses of the scientist and to testing in a laboratory.

Do these biological facts about the way material cells act have meaning far beyond the purely physical? Certainly they stimulate our exploration of philosophical and theological facts as well. But, back to our quest: The destiny of the ovum is either to be fertilized or to die. In either case it ceases to exist as a germ cell. A similar destiny of the sperm is to be fertilized or to die. In fertilization, the germ cells lose their identity and fill their destiny. The result is a new individual, with a new life, a new unique identity, and a new destiny. A new creation!

To illustrate the unique importance of this new individual, let us look at you. When did your life begin? Simply go back in time. Before you were an adult, you were an adolescent, and before that a child, and before then, an infant. Before you were an infant, i.e., before you were born, you were a fetus, and before that, an embryo. Before you were an embryo, around the time of your implantation, you were a blastocyst, and before that a morula, and before that, a zygote or fertilized ovum—a speck smaller than a period. However, you were never a sperm or an unfertilized ovum!

Therefore, while life and its humanness or humanity are continuous, your unique individual human life began when the nucleus of your father's sperm fused with the nucleus of your mother's ovum—at conception! So we see that there is something important, something special that occurs at conception. A new life, a new human life, a new individual, a new human being begins!

The term human being is used interchangeably with human individual which is frequently shortened to just individual. It signifies a complete, though not completed, living, organized, unique individual human organism, always more or less dependent on other human beings, but always with a certain amount of autonomy in charge of its own destiny.

The zygote, i.e., the fertilized ovum or conceptus, fits all of these criteria. This fundamentally complete cell has an information content equivalent to a one thousand volume set of *Encyclopedia Britannica* and unlike that of any other human being. The new cell is programmed to divide; differentiate; form hormones and enzymes; implant; develop organs, brain, nerve and bone; eventually becoming an adult and able to repeat the reproductive cycle.

Thus, Ingelman-Sundberg and Wirsen write: "When does an embryo in a human mother become a human being? It has been one all the time, since the moment of conception." These answers are as well established and completely objective as any that science has to offer. These facts are not a matter of theological belief or philosophical theories. They are the expression of reality as determined by scientific observation and analysis. To deny this is to lose touch with reality.

The philosopher Germain Grisez, in summarizing his study of the scientific literature on the subject, states: "The sex cells are formed from the living matter of man and woman; the sex cells are themselves alive." And so the result of a union does not really come to life but simply comes to be a unified life—a new individual.

A senate judiciary committee held hearings from 23 April to 18 June 1981 on a bill, S-158—the Human Life Bill, which seeks to define when human life begins. The report of these hearings concluded that contemporary scientific evidence points to a clear conclusion: The life of a human being begins at conception. That overwhelming majority of scientists agree that conception marks the beginning of the life of a human being, a being that is alive and a member of the human species. This biological consensus has been confirmed by the process of creating a new human life outside the mother—the *test tube baby*. [According to] LeJeune: A new human being will emerge only from the encounter of the ovum and sperm.

These hearings also distinguished and examined the scientific question and the value question. They found that we must consider not only that unborn children are human beings, but also whether to accord their lives intrinsic worth and value equal to those of other human beings. The two questions are separate and distinct. It is a scientific question whether an unborn child is a human being in the sense of living members of the human species. It is a value question whether the life of an unborn child has intrinsic worth and equal value.

They concluded:

> Science can tell us whether a being is alive and a member of the human species. It cannot tell us whether to accord value to that being. The government of any society, however, that accords intrinsic worth to all human life must make two determinations: 1) a factual determination in recognizing the existence of all human beings, and 2) a value decision affirming the worth of human life.

To Recapitulate:

The kind of life applicable to discussion of abortion in a pluralistic society is biological life. Biological life does not begin, it is continuous. A cell can come only from one or more living cells. The biological criteria of human lives is the genetic constitution of the cells and in their origin.

The quality of being human does not begin—it is continuous. A human cell can come only from one or more living human cells. A biological life of an individual begins at fertilization. From that time until death, the individual is never anything but alive, never anything but human. He is a human being.

These facts are not matters of religion or opinion or theory. They are the results of scientific observation. The knowledgeable members of the medical profession are in agreement. Thus, the International Code of Medical Ethics states: "A doctor must always bear in mind the importance of preserving human life from the time of conception until death." Similarly, the Declaration of Geneva reads: "I will maintain the utmost respect for human life from the time of conception."

Abortion, then, must be the taking of human life. That such is the case is candidly admitted in an editorial in the pro-abortion journal, *California Medicine*:

> The reverence of each and every human life has been a keystone of western medicine and is the ethic which has caused physicians to try to preserve, protect, repair, prolong, and enhance every human life. Since the old ethic has not been fully displaced, it has been necessary to separate the idea of abortion from the idea of killing which continues to be socially abhorrent. The result has been a curious avoidance of the scientific fact, which everyone really knows, that human life begins at conception, and is continuous, whether intra- or extra-uterine until death. The very considerable semantic gymnastics which are required to rationalize abortion as anything but taking a human life would be ludicrous if they were not often put forth under socially impeccable auspices. This suggests that this schizophrenic sort of subterfuge is necessary because, while a new ethic is being accepted, the old one has not yet been rejected.

In summary, the answer to our question, *when does human life begin?* is a scientific answer—an individual human life begins at conception. Hence, abortion kills human life. The value question remains. *When, if ever, can this killing be justified?* There is no *absolute* right to life. *But*, it remains the *fundamental* right that is the basis of all other human rights, including liberty and justice.

Our culture and our society have traditionally justified the killing of human life in three areas: 1) self-defense; 2) war, and 3) capital punishment. In 1973, in weighing the rights of the mother versus the rights of the unborn child, the Supreme Court created new rules for justifiable homicide!

Appendix B

A Pro-life Perspective on Abortion

In 1990, I was involved in a pediatrician's conference in Houston. I gave this speech in defense of the right to life of unborn children.

In the United States today, there are 1,500,000 abortions performed yearly, over 4,000 daily. Since 1973 and *Roe v. Wade*, an estimated 25,000,000-plus abortions have been performed.

Presently, nearly one of every three humans conceived in this country are aborted. Ninety-five to 98 percent are done on normal, healthy women with normal, healthy babies for nonmedical reasons. The remaining 2 percent to 5 percent are for rape, incest, eugenics, or specific medical reasons, i.e., the mother's life or serious health risks. Late abortions, during the second or third trimester, are an estimated 150,000 annually, or one of every ten abortions.

The liberty, the freedom, to choose abortion as a constitutional right to privacy declared in *Roe* is for all practical purposes unlimited. Judicial decisions have granted the right of the mother to abort, or separate herself from the pre-born infant, at any stage of pregnancy, for any reason, or no reason at all, as a matter of personal privacy and individual choice—unlimited maternal autonomy.

The creation of the right was one of the most radical in the civilized world. The constitutional protection of the life of the pre-born was repealed by judicial fiat, the constitution amended, and a new provision written, the right to abortion. The representative legislative process which is designed to deal with such vital moral and social issues was entirely circumvented by unprecedented judicial activism.

The abortion decisions have had massive personal and social consequences. The abortion rights issue continues unabated. It divides the nation and divides us as pediatricians. Many profess to be pro-choice, but choice is not the issue, abortion is. In reality, you can only be pro-life or pro-abortion. I appreciate very much the opportunity to present the pro-life view.

Legalized as a *private* act, abortion has become the *public* issue that compels almost everyone to take a stand. Human sexual activity and reproductive rights may be exercised in private, but they are manifestly moral acts with social consequences. Abortion is not a private act. It involves not only the mother and the unborn infant, but the father, an abortionist, a clinic or hospital staff, rules and regulations, constant litigation and legislation regarding public funding, etc.

The liberty has adversely intruded into human relationships. The legal structure of the family is in disarray. Minor children are granted autonomy in the abortion decision. The father has no right to protect the pre-born child as its progenitor. The greatest social consequence of all has been the destruction of human life. The hard cases of abortion cannot compare in number and tragedy with the social fact that Americans are now wasting their own on a scale exceeding war.

[There is] disinformation, in the form of dehumanization of the unborn child, for example, blob of tissue, or product of conception, or fetus not baby and, euphemistic misrepresentations of the relationships of morality and the law, for example, [you] cannot legislate morality, or just a matter of personal choice. Such disinformation has limited the analysis of abortion to a political debate regarding freedom of choice and the right to privacy of the mother. An honest evaluation would be to also analyze the issue from at least four other perspectives: 1) biological; 2) morality: ethics and the law; 3) societal; 4) philosophical.

Abortion and Human Life: The Biological Perspective

It is a scientific fact that an individual life begins at conception. Briefly reflect on ourselves. When did your human life, your being a human, begin? Simply go back in *time*. Before you were an adult, you were an adolescent, and before that a child, and before that an infant. Before you were an infant, you were a fetus, and, before that, an embryo. Before that, you were a zygote or fertilized ovum. Manipulation of the unique new DNA of the human zygote records that the life code for each feature of you as a new individual was present at conception. Individuation is clearly demonstrated at the three-cell stage from which each individual builds the self. The genetic code transmits information which will animate matter. It is the force directing matter to form a new human being. In vitro fertilization (IVF) cogently confirms conception as the beginning of a new individual, with a unique identity, a new creation.

There is, indeed, a mystical quality to conception as the crossroad between matter, energy, and information. Human beings call other entirely new human beings into existence through the material information that relates parents to children and generation to generation.

Abortion: The Moral Perspective

Abortion is a profound issue of morality, both private and public. Our attitude toward abortion mirrors our personal and social respect for, and behavior toward, human life and humanity. Is the new conception human? Humanity is not acquired. There is no humanization process; you either are or you are not. Humanity is innate. We do not ask the question of any other species. The question only arises when dealing with human beings that we want to discriminate against. Witness black slavery and the Jewish Holocaust. To justify the atrocities against them, they first had to be dehumanized, that is, nonhuman means nonperson. Abortion is the taking of innocent human life. To justify abortion, the human life has to be dehumanized or devalued.

What value has that life? Is the human life a human being having intrinsic worth and inherent value? Is the human being a person? Is personhood an inherent value of being, a human being, or does personhood depend on ones function? Age? Level of development? Achievement? Quality of life? If so, who decides? How?

Does the new, genetically complete, unique individual formed at conception have any right to life? Our society presumes that there is a fundamental right to life of all persons. However, this fundamental right is not absolute. The right to life is limited. As a society, we justify homicide—the killing of persons—in self-defense, war, and capital punishment. There is, however, the firmly held notion that life remains a fundamental right. It is the basis of all other human rights, including freedom and justice.

Thus, the personhood of the pre-born infant and its right to life, *not* the privacy right of the mother, is the seminal moral issue in the abortion debate. This is the reason pro-abortionists frantically deny the humanity of the pre-born. The alpha, or the fetus, was dehumanized and devalued, lost its personhood and its right to life.

Distinctions are to be made between a human life, a human being, and a human person. Human life may be a cell, tissue, organ, etc., while a human being is a biologic individual of the species. When does biologic life become an individual person with human rights? In the pro-life view, human personhood begins at conception. A fully programmed individual is present whose personhood is already there unfolding and developing from within. It is an actual person, with potential, not a potential person. All human beings are persons! To deny personhood to a biological human being is unjust!

Conception is the dividing line. You are the same being from conception on and an actual person through each stage of the life cycle. Since human personhood begins at conception, abortion is the direct killing of a person. Abortion is feticide.

The Supreme Court separated the idea of abortion from the idea of killing a person by declaring the pre-born a nonperson. Personhood, for legal purposes, was determined by judges to begin at birth. The pre-born infant was rendered a nonperson, and, therefore, the mother bears no moral or legal responsibility for her child to be born, unless wanted. This decision was premised on the moral judgment that the personhood of the human being is a matter of function. Hence, the abortion morality is based on the belief that all human beings are not persons. The court declared the fetus a human nonperson because it is not functionally viable outside of the womb.

Furthermore, the court, acting on the ethical concept of competing interests, claims, and rights, judged the mother's right to privacy and choice superseded any right of the fetus to life. Its life depends on the mother's choice to carry the fetus to viability and birth.

For the first time in our nation, innocent, individual human life is taken, not for specific reasons, such as the life of the mother, rape, incest, or handicap, but for subjective, vague personal and social reasons.

The functional definition of personhood is appropriate for scientific purposes or prediction and experimentation, but is not adequate or appropriate for moral reasoning or social constructs. Ordinary reason and common sense distinguishes between what one is and what one does; between being a person and functioning as a person. A robot functions as a person, but it is not a person because functioning is only one aspect of being a person.

Equating one's performance or achievement level with personhood justifies existence by measuring one's utility or quality of life. This subjective appraisal of human beings in various stages of life can be dehumanizing with eventual disastrous social consequences. A relative scale of measuring humanity and personhood is preliminary to inhumanity. How do you wish to be valued? For who you are? Or for what you do?

Can we ethically justify abortion for any reason other than the mother's competing right to life? Since we now have biological proof of the fact that human life begins at conception, and, a graphic awareness from fetology of the substantive nature of the pre-born child, would it not seem reasonable that the choice of abortion be limited?

What interventions that abridge maternal autonomy are justified for the pre-born's protection from harm? What of ethical constraints and legal sanctions for maternal substance abuse? Of toxic exposure? Of damaging infections such as STDs and AIDS? What of growing a fetus to provide donor tissue or organs?

Why are we treating the pre-born, medically and surgically, as a patient, if it is a nonperson? Recently, in San Francisco, an unborn child was partially removed from the womb in order to have a renal tract obstruction repaired. After the surgery, he was replaced in the womb to continue the pregnancy. Was he a person while out of the womb and then a nonperson again when he was replaced? Or, since the procedure involves the delivery of the lower half of the body, did he achieve personhood for his buttocks but not for his brain? These are the scientific anomalies of the Supreme Court decision. No wonder Justice O'Connor has said that *Roe v. Wade* is on a collision course with itself.

What of the rights of the frozen embryo and the

responsibility of the mother? What value the commodity of the surrogate mother? What is our responsibility to the pre-born infant? To the father? To the family? To society? What are the state's legitimate interests in reproduction and the common good, if not that of the pre-born infant? There is a valid moral, ethical basis for limiting maternal autonomy: the best interests of the unborn child and its right to life.

Abortion: The Social Perspective

Elective abortion impassions all of the *human life* issues, i.e., infanticide, euthanasia, condoned/assisted suicide, and, also, the *human relationship* issues, i.e., the structure of marriage and the family, the role and duty of parents, the limitations of the paternal procreator, the virtue that characterizes a mother, inter-generational relationships, indeed, community itself. We are individual moral agents but also obligate social beings.

Part of the public controversy is intractable. The debate depends on basic personal assumptions and judgments about the nature of human life and human relationships. In addition, the reality of what happens to the pre-born infant in abortion elicits a response much greater than its physical size. The palpable evidence of the living pre-born child not previously accessible to perception is now vividly portrayed by fetoscopy and ultrasound. This evidence is clearly sufficient to erase any doubt of the fetus' identifiable humanity.

The pre-born's substantive nature, its humanity, and personhood has been obscured because of the reluctance to confront the reality as well as the *politicization* of the alpha as a social engineering problem and a woman's liberation issue, i.e., sexual and reproductive freedom. Few, if any, state that abortion is a good in the abstract, but claim that it is a necessity in our land of sexual freedom, imperfect contraception, and limited resources. This suggests that the real issue is sex, not abortion.

The acceptance of the personal-social practice of elective abortion, not because it is *good* but because pro-abortionists can see no valid alternative, is unethical. Pro-abortionists know it is morally wrong but approve of it anyway.

There are many specious arguments for permissive abortion, such as overpopulation; social problems; cost benefit; unwanted; it's only a tissue anyway, not viable; coat-hangers, back alleys; adoption no option; and, of course, privacy rights, control over one's own body, reproductive freedom to choose. Let us focus on the latter first, the slogan of choice as justification for permissive abortion.

The freedom of choice—choice to do what? To kill or not to kill the alpha and the right to privacy. But this involves two bodies, two lives are involved! Permissive abortion is not simply a matter of private morality because fundamental principles of justice are involved. In reality, the reproductive right is the freedom to have sex. The reproductive choice is to have sexual intercourse or not. Once with child the right has been exercised, and the choice has been made. The choice now is childbirth and life, or abortion and death, i.e., to be the mother of a live baby or a dead baby.

Anyway, all choices are not justifiable as a matter of privacy and protected as a right. The choice may be good or bad, right or wrong, depending on what act is chosen. Abortion and childbirth are not morally equivalent: Abortion is destructive of life; childbirth is giving of life. Control over one's body includes other options besides abortion, i.e., sexual continence, contraception, voluntary sterilization, and adoption. No one has absolute control over his own body, for example, there are legal sanctions to limit prostitution, drug abuse, and suicide. Is individual responsibility and self-control to be replaced by abortion? There is no absolute freedom. There is no freedom which may not be constitutionally restricted or regulated. What of the alpha's choice?

Other specious arguments are:

Overpopulation. The teeming masses concept requires abortion as a back-up contraception. The United States is not overpopulated and faces significant demographic problems. If overpopulation is valid, who should be eliminated? The aged? The poor? The dependent chronically ill or handicapped? Killing is not an acceptable solution to population problems.

Panacea for Social Problems. Abortion-on-demand has proceeded apace for seventeen years. Yet, the personal and social problems of women, children, and families mount geometrically with increased welfare rolls, poverty, illegitimacy, and child abuse. Could it be that abortion is a part of the problem?

Cost Benefit. The body count mentality asserts abortion is cheaper than childbirth and pragmatically eliminates the alpha as good economics and politics. A dehumanizing concept which readily applies to other classes of citizens.

Unwanted. Every child ought to be a wanted child, and, if not wanted, eliminated. There is a myth that if [a child is] unwanted, social evils result. Pregnancies may be unwanted but children are wanted and adoption is a reasonable option.

The fetus is mere tissue *and* all are alike. The alpha is an individual living human being, residing with the mother and is distinct and unique in its function and bodily features.

Viability. In vitro fertilization moves the date of viability back to conception. Simply put, the pre-born is viable unless aborted. Should the pre-born's youth deprive it of the right to life? A pre-born baby is an individual human being, regardless of viability.

Coat Hangers/Back Alleys. There was a precipitous drop in deaths prior to legalization [of abortion] due to improved medical care. The legality of abortion has had no significant effect on reported deaths due to abortion. The abortion procedure has been revolutionized and the medical risks of abortion—legal or illegal—are minimal, that is, for the mother. Today, legal abortion deaths have replaced the illegal ones. If abortion were outlawed, there would be a reduction in abortions performed and abortion deaths.

Adoption. Pro-abortionists depict adoption as an unutterable tragedy. For whom? The very questionable psychological harm to the mother refused abortion still does not refute, or weaken, the fact that the alpha is a human life.

For those who have reconciled themselves to the hard reality of a society regulating reproduction by abortion, I would ask: Is it compatible with our knowledge, our understanding, our values, our beliefs, and our collective wisdom? Of our sense of humanity? Can we honestly redefine and mask the reality of the alpha by simply categorizing abortion as a private choice? The abortion liberty does not have a legitimate foundation in the constitution or constitutional principle. Its basis lies in politics and the sexual/social revolution. It is sustained by invalid assumptions and myths which convey the necessity of the freedom. The liberty of abortion is not a human good and infringes on the rights of the alpha as well as others and has serious moral and social consequences.

Abortion laws were not the result of religious dogma, were not invented by men to control women and children as male property, and were not aimed at discriminating against the poor. Abortion laws were to protect the unborn child based on biological knowledge and respect for life and human rights.

The language of the liberty to abort and its masking by the media is designed to eliminate from discourse the living nature of the being who is aborted. Those opposing the liberty are depicted as male chauvinists, or uninstructed traditionalists, or religious bigots, or hypocritical enemies of the poor. Those championing the liberty are portrayed as high-minded idealists who declare the foundation of the liberty to be as follows: 1) the insignificant nature of the fetal being; 2) personhood begins at birth, and 3) the privacy of the pregnant woman to unlimited maternal autonomy.

This is a shaky foundation! A human life begins at conception and the substantive character of the alpha is clearly manifest while an *unlimited* right to abortion based on privacy has no basis in ethics or law. The integration of the abortion ethic and the abortion experience into the morality of our culture has failed. It is impossible to reconcile what is done in an abortion with basic norms.

We intuitively reject the direct killing of the alpha and cannot reconcile abortion with the overarching prohibition against the taking of human life. Life has always been an overriding value and the sanctity of life is not a theological tenet but a secular concept. It is our moral duty to each other. Abortion functions as a symbol of infidelity, of destruction, and the killing of the alpha is understood as inherently evil. In the body politic, the separation of abortion from the idea of killing is not accepted and abortion should be limited.

Seventeen years of elective abortion, along with no-fault sex and divorce, has not solved the social problems or met the needs of women and children. The rate of dependency associated with the failure of marriage and fractured families poses a monumental threat to civil life and the health and welfare of increasing numbers of women and children. Many are moved to ask if we are committing *social suicide*.

Abortion is a deadly failure. It has failed to achieve its personal, social, economic, political, or cultural promises. The values to be cherished, i.e., human life, child bearing, parental fidelity, etc., are values with religious origins but exist in humanism.

The impossibility of reconciling the present liberty of abortion requires its eventual limitation. The liberty lacks a valid ethical basis, has no constitutional foundation, and is premised on failed social policy and discredited sexual politics.

What is effective to restrict abortion liberty? Pregnancy is not a disease. Pro-abortionists pretend that there are no alternatives to elective abortion. The pro-life view is that there are many adequate, valid alternatives, i.e., sexual continence, contraception, voluntary sterilization, adoption, as well as crisis pregnancy management, and, social and medical support services. These sustain ethical values of human life and protection of those killed by abortion, women exploited by abortion and those fulfilled by adoption. The American Academy of Pediatrics and its members are presently vigorously supporting access to adequate medical care of the indigent and needy, especially as it affects the most vulnerable and dependent, i.e., pregnant women, children, and youth. What of the AAP's responsibility to the pre-born?

Abortion: The Philosophical Perspective

Surely you must share some of my concern for the subjective viewpoint regarding human life, particularly in the face of the developing economic constraints on medical care, for example, AIDS. Utilitarian needs can provide enormous pressure to alter physicians' mindset regarding human life. What will become of human freedom and justice in the emerging context of biotechnology, the relativistic quality of life ethic and utilitarian mandates? Death resolves many personal and social problems, but killing creates many more. I am convinced that physicians should and must speak against escalating death solutions. I seek your support in opposing death options, i.e., abortion-on-demand, infanticide, euthanasia, and condoned/assisted suicide as means to solve personal and socioeconomic problems. Much more worthy alternatives are available to our profession and our society in positively addressing human need and values.

Efforts to encourage death solutions to social and medical problems, especially of the pre-born child, the terminally ill, the elderly, the disabled, the demented, the insane, the suicidal, the handicapped, the chronically ill, the dependent, or the simply burdensome and useless eaters represents social Darwinism. The use of death solutions will reflect how, as a culture, we turn from efforts to improve our lives together to the lesser good of helping each other die. Let us seek to diminish pain, share pain, but respect the value of life.

Leon Kass cautions individuals and society to consider the power over reproduction with its risks of voluntary dehumanization. The use of knowledge to remove causes of dehumanization such as disease, starvation, violence, etc., are to be valued, but the use of knowledge as power, uninformed by wisdom, can render us irreversibly dehumanized. What of the dehumanizing consequences of elective abortion, no-fault sexuality and divorce, and programmed reproduction along with child-rearing given over to the child care centers, the schools, the media and the state? These alternatives are designed to manage procreation, but at what cost? If we accept the killing of a healthy pre-born infant for trivial reasons, why not the abnormal newborn infant who is now unwanted? C.S. Lewis mused: "In the end, the price of relieving man's estate might well be the abolition of man."

The present status of unrestricted abortion-on-demand for vague personal, social, not specific, medical reasons represents child abuse in a most unconscionable public form. Significantly and predictably, we find mounting death solution proposals that represent an inadequate basis for the ethical practice of medicine. Standards such as unworthy, unwanted, not meaningful, wrongful, unfulfilling, are subjective not objective criteria and inadequate in principle.

The new ethic for the conduct of medical practice has, and can, lead to enormous inhumanities in the name of being humane, compassionate. Recall Binding's essay of 1920 entitled, *The Release of the Destruction of Life Devoid of Value*. This formed the philosophical, ethical, and legal basis to justify Nazi pogroms. Physicians must remain committed to caring, not killing, and not serve as social executioners. We must speak out against the emerging death philosophy of a materialistic, hedonistic society with an elitist bent. As caring professionals, committed to the value of human life, we must be positive moral agents.

The [American] Academy of Pediatrics stood in the breech on the issue of infanticide. There are *two* persons in the abortion issue. The humanity and personhood of the pre-born is objective reality. As pediatricians, I believe we must speak up for children, all children, including the pre-born, the unwanted, and the imperfect, while advocating valid alternatives for the mother's care and well-being. Both patients, mother and child, have an equal right to life, mutual care, and respect.

Summary

In the pro-life view, individual human life, a human being, a person, and its viability commence at conception. Protection for the new *human person*, is a profound matter of morality and crucial to a just society. Justifiable homicide, the legal taking of the life of a human person, is limited. The taking of the life of a pre-born baby is justifiable only when the life of the mother is at risk.

The view that killing of the pre-born baby is justifiable for personal and social reasons, not specific medical reasons, based on the concept of choice, i.e., unlimited maternal autonomy, is unethical and should be limited by legal sanctions.

Conclusions

Scientifically, the alpha is an independent individual human life which begins at conception and represents a sound humanistic basis on which to limit abortion.

Ethically, abortion is justified only for clearly defined medical necessity, i.e., the life and serious health risk of the mother.

Legally, the right to life of the unborn child warrants legal sanctions that limit abortion.

Philosophically, death, as a solution to personal and

social problems, represents social Darwinism and dehumanization. Physicians should be committed to caring, not killing, and protecting the equal right to life as the basis of human freedom and justice.

Appendix C

Suicide: Any Limits to Self-Autonomy?

I gave this speech at an American Academy of Pediatrics meeting in New York in April 1992.

Introduction

The moral values and behavior—the morality—emerging in our culture in recent decades is based on the fundamental notion of the individual's autonomy in ethical decision-making. This *principle* of doing ethics can be stated as a simple proposition: One may behave in any way one chooses, and it is ethical, as long as one does not do harm to others.

This ethical decision-making process in our varied and diverse culture is termed the *pluralistic* proposition, i.e., those acts that are personal and private and are not harmful to others should be left to individual choice. Morality becomes simply a matter of the individual's choice, independent of any moral judgment of the choice, as to good or bad, right or wrong. Thus, occurs the privatization of morality as an expression of individualism, and values are relative, simply a matter of individual choice—moral relativism.

Dan Callahan in the October 1981 *Hastings Center Report* termed these new values the minimalist ethic and questioned their validity as well as their adequacy to sustain a viable culture, in particular during hard times. He asks,

> has the pluralistic proposition derived from John Stuart Mill's *On Liberty* been distorted in its adoption by our culture? Mill's principle was to govern the legal relationship between the individual and the state, not the individual's personal moral life.

In the language of individual rights that frames the autonomy principle of doing ethics, the only judgment permitted on moral autonomy is to assess harm to others. If no harm is discerned, we must suspend moral judgment, and if we fail to suspend that judgment, we are guilty of abridging the individual's right to privacy and self-determination.

The question of moral valuing, doing ethics, now becomes *what, if anything, is the community entitled to define as harm to others?* Can a change in the moral environment, for example, in personal and social attitudes toward sex, marriage, and family be considered harmful? Or does the right to privacy, as unlimited personal autonomy, free the individual from moral regulation, from communal standards, and best expressed in the pejorative statement, "Don't put your values on me!" Even though we are *obligate* moral beings acting in a social context, we are enjoined to be nonjudgmental.

Harm to others as the sole test of the morality of a person's choice provides no substantive basis for judging personal morality. If individual choice is the basis of ethical decision-making, then the issue is placed outside the sphere of human reason, moral persuasion, and legal restriction. One person's morality being as good as another's, the community may not adopt moral standards (the concept that you cannot legislate morality).

Conversely, this ethic of moral autonomy provides no sustenance for those moral values that do require limited autonomy—for example, duty, self-sacrifice, responsibility to others, altruism, the common good, transcendent values rather than private values, and future needs rather than present desires. Dr. Callahan depicts our culture today as striving to sanctify the moral autonomous individual as the ideal, denying communal goals, ultimate ends become procedural safe-guards, and, ignores human meaning and purpose, or, assigns these matters to hidden private lives.

Though liberating, is individual autonomy an adequate ethic to sustain a valid human society? Or, does the lack of personal moral limits to individual autonomy constitute individual as well as social pathology?

Autonomous ethical decision-making produces a morality that enthrones the transcendence of the individual over the community because autonomy is the highest human good and voluntary informed consent is the contract model of human relationships. Callahan asks, "Does our cultural experiment of the past twenty-five years represent a slide into moral indifference, callous self-interest, and wanton violence?"

I will seek to analyze the limits of autonomy in ethical decision-making as to the current seminal ethical issues, condoned and/or assisted suicide—active voluntary euthanasia.

Suicide and Voluntary Euthanasia: The Problem

Suicide is the leading cause of death in our society, striking the most vulnerable—the very old, the sick, and the young—and, it is rapidly becoming *the* issue as to a right and a choice. There is an epidemic of suicide, particularly in the age group fifteen to twenty-four years, the adolescent and young adult. This is the only age group in this country with a rising death rate, mostly due to suicide, homicide, and accidents. Suicide is second only to accidental death as a cause of death in this age group. The CDC reported that one of twelve American high-school students (grades nine to twelve)—or, nearly 276,000 teen-agers—tried to commit suicide and one in four seriously contemplated it. Of those attempting, one in four sustained serious injury and four to five thousand youngsters per year die suicidally. Death due to suicide in this age group has tripled in the past decades. In fact, much of the adolescent accidental death incidence is believed to be suicide. There are an additional 25,000 suicides per year in older age groups. Ninety-three percent of these suicides are depression/alcohol related and only 2 to 6 percent are terminally ill. The vast majority who commit suicide are in good physical health, including 67 percent of elderly suicides.

Indeed, we have a health problem of significant proportions demanding serious consideration as to intervention, but, even more important, prevention. Additionally, a sense of urgency is justified by the best-selling status of Derek Humphry's *Final Exit*, Dr. Jack Kevorkian's suicide machine, the Dutch euthanasia experience, the AIDS epidemic, and legislative initiatives which would legalize the active role of the doctor in physician-assisted suicide. Now that successful deliverance is available to anyone who can read, the success rate in suicide is expected to increase.

The Ethical Issue

Suicide and assisted suicide are psycho-social and bioethical issues of huge import today. Unfortunately, these issues are often trivialized in the media which tends to glorify suicide, and educational activities invite a growing interest in the proposition that suicide can be rational and, therefore, justifiable. In essence, this constitutes an effort to achieve public acceptance of suicide as a fundamental, individual right of personal autonomy for everyone. In addition, voluntary euthanasia, i.e., condoned and/or assisted suicide, is actively affirmed and progressively accepted by emotional and intellectual conditioning, thereby providing the basis for moral acceptance of the legalization of a claim *right to suicide*, a right to kill one's self and to be assisted in exercising that right (the right to die and the right to choose death).

Socially and *culturally*, suicide is viewed in the context of overpopulation, inadequate care and costs, thereby becoming a matter of social utility where suicidal death is to be accepted, encouraged, and protected as a solution to personal and social problems.

Personal acceptance of a right to suicide *psychologically* represents a heightened consciousness about death that is intrinsic to the adaptation of the potentially suicidal individual to suicidal behavior. Add to this the social and cultural acceptance of the utility of suicidal death and an increase of such death and morbidity, particularly in vulnerable minors and young adults, the sick, disabled, elderly, poor, chronically ill, criminal, etc., inevitably follows. Thoughtful people ask: "Could this be the clarion call for euthanasia as a solution to personal, social, and economic problems of the dependent and burdensome?"

Those who view any limits on the right to suicide as abrogating an individual, fundamental moral right of self-determination also declare that the right to self-determination has no social consequences. The morality of the issue, both in the spheres of ethics and law, is cast in the language of rights. In particular, the Millean view of absolute autonomy, i.e., suicide is purely personal, a matter of autonomy, individual choice, and the right to privacy, i.e., control over one's own body.

An Ethical Analysis of Suicide

The effort to develop criteria for permissible suicide and assisted suicide is based on quality-of-life criteria such as terminal illness, pain, chronic illness, handicap, burden, and philosophic, legalistic grounds that reflect the acceptance of suicide-on-demand. Such approaches to suicide simply ignore the meaning of suicidal ideation and behavior, i.e., the individual's adaptation to life. *Psychodynamically*, the potential suicidal personality reflects an interaction of the role of depression, the impact of intimacy, and the individual's self-identity within the social circumstances, i.e., crime, violence, drugs, alcohol, sexual expression, etc. Consequently, the potential for the suicidal act is culturally determined and its expression relative as to various motives and methods. Thus, the error and potential abuse of socially sanctioned suicide is enormous! In particular, emotionally vulnerable minors and young adults are peculiarly at risk to suicidal ideation and behavior.

Ethically, this younger age group lacks competence as to this decision-making process, as well as knowledge, perception, and experience. In fact, most are incapable of true, informed consent and therefore lack the power to say *yes* or *no*. They are characteristically impulse-driven, implicitly coerced, ambivalent, readily manipulated, subject to irrational anger and fantasies as well as depression. Their functional character is immature, at risk of altered judgment, and a narrow consideration of alternatives. In sum, adolescents and young adults lack the competence, adequate informed consent, and true freedom to make such a choice of finality while subject to coercive, manipulative cultural determinants.

However, the ethical principle for condoned/assisted suicide is now in vogue, that is, the philosophic rationale of autonomy, privacy, control over one's body, and, self-determination that suicide is a right and a choice. The science, *suicidology*, is also now available to anyone who can read and, thus, the principle can readily be put into practice. Legitimate concern arises in view of the advocacy agenda of the Hemlock Society and the euthanasia movement. It is noteworthy that the Society for the Right to Die has been renamed Choice-in-Dying. Thus, euphemistically, the issue becomes not *who dies?* but *who decides?*; not *what is done to whom?* but *who makes the choice?* Hereby, the issue, aid-in-dying, is relegated to process and procedural safeguards. The true substantive issue, however, is not choice but suicide. To condone suicide and assisted suicide, is accepting active voluntary euthanasia as ethical. Self-deliverance and death from the doctor's helping hand is mercy-killing, active euthanasia, and we have crossed the line.

Ethical Analysis of Choice

[Dr. Daniel] Callahan recently (November 1990) voiced an ethical challenge to pro-choice advocates. How can it make sense to favor the right to choice but to be morally indifferent—amoral—about the use of that right? What are the appropriate ethical uses of choice? Presuming no harm to others, what of the other aspect of the pluralistic proposition, the morality of the choice made? The autonomy argument removes all criteria for evaluating the choice, except that it be uncoerced.

Choice is only the beginning of morality and does not end until a justifiable choice has been made on some reasonably serious basis, not patent self-interest. Is it possible to hold that choice should simply be left to the individual and, at the same time, assume that such a serious decision is always a morally justifiable choice? Are we to leave the choice to the individual though the choice be a grave one, worthy of public as well as private reflection? The glorification of the principle of a right to die and a right to privacy—the choice ethic—also ignores the obvious fact that people make choices harmful to themselves, to others and/or to society. If we empower choice rights at all costs, do we ignore the harm and deny the protective rights for the individual, other individuals, and the community?

These questions are crucial for many other ethical debates regarding private choices and personal morality. The cost of failing to take seriously the personal moral issues involved in individual choice is a basic threat to moral honesty. There are insistent moral issues in the ethics of autonomy and unlimited choice.

A vital pluralism actively debates the content of private choice as it would public choice. Autonomy, privacy-rights advocates either seek social solutions at the expense of moral soundness or they choose to consider social issues of far greater importance than private moral issues. This warrants serious concern about the very nature of the pluralistic proposition. All choices are not justifiable as a matter of personal privacy and protected as a right. The choice may be good or bad, right or wrong, depending on what is chosen.

The idea that we can draw a sharp line between the public and private spheres of morality, between public choice and private choice, is untenable. Private choice is shaped, even determined, by the societal context. For credibility and the common good, a robust debate of the personal morality of individual choice must be undertaken. Can self-determination, suicide, and assisted suicide be justified as simply a matter of individual choice?

Discussion

Those factors helping potential suicidal people want to live, i.e., the sacred value of human life and the notion that death decisions are not ours to make, are waning in our society. Fear of the next world, whether or not it is still a factor in people's private lives, certainly does not enter into the current secular wisdom and practice which frames the issue in the language of autonomy, futility of treatment and nurturing care, and cost containment.

There are dangers, but, also vital safeguards, in attempting to limit certain individual moral decisions. In particular, bio-ethical/psycho-social issues such as suicide and assisted suicide require drawing arbitrary lines. Should hard cases determine philosophy, ethics, and the law? Though not fashionable, the protection of certain values requires risk, even heroism, because it is a matter of greater injustice. A pertinent example is guerrilla warfare and the military rule of no direct attacks on noncombatants. Hereby a soldier risks his life in order to prevent the killing of the innocent. Similarly, in the issue of self-termination, Meehan commends our commitment to diminishing pain, sharing pain, but protecting the value of life. Thus, we sustain certain moral principles or values by drawing arbitrary lines even at the risk of limiting individual rights and autonomy.

Individual rights and personal autonomy are not without reasonable limits as to choice. We need to protect potential victims, in particular the vulnerable of all ages, by limiting the individual right to suicide. Limits to suicide are necessary because there is harm to the individual, to other individuals, and to the community.

Conceptually, the view that the nature of decision-making in self-termination is simply measuring life on a balance scale is erroneous. That life is merely a matter of a balance sheet as to an individual risk/gain ratio versus a social cost/benefit ratio represents an illusion of control, omnipotent control, and a delusion of the self that suicide is beautiful, a perfect mode of death when, in fact, it is a desperate and unhappy resolution of painful conflicts. Suicidal ideation is antithetical to pleasure and life—both individual and communal.

Dr. Will Gaylin points out that individual rights, such as the right to suicide, depend on their social significance and man's obligate duty and responsibility. The premise of individual rights is appropriate as to social justice but other issues, such as the right to suicide, resist this approach. Therefore, it is crucial to modify rights arguments on behalf of responsibility, decency, and relationships and recognize the right to limit individual autonomy. Not just in terms of the state interest, but beyond to values and institutions that are essential to the individual and individualism.

Furthermore, Dr. Gaylin pleads for a more communitarian approach to human problems and points out the necessity to draw arbitrary lines in such moral and psycho-social issues. He recommends that we not overvalue that which is deficient in our society and not view all issues in terms of the ill we are trying to correct, especially the hard cases such as terminal, painful illness. He points out that rights advocates can live with a pure conscience if they keep their focus on social justice issues since rights talk only becomes significant when we see a conflict of rights in a hierarchy of competing values. Thus, a right to suicide has to be balanced against other moral priorities, i.e., respect for certain moral principles even at the risk of individual rights and personal autonomy. Values which should be high in priority are life itself, health, family, community, and down the line, rights of autonomy, dignity, and privacy.

Leon Kass declares that rational suicide is a sophism. He contends that suicide on demand is not rational or justifiable, is unethical, and should not be legal. To quote:

> It is not pure reason that finds life unbearable. The dominant motives are fear, resignation and despair, or, in other words, the desire to escape. The utter rationalization of life under the banner of the will, seeking mastery of nature and the conquest of death, leads only to dehumanization. Modern rationalism, being morally neutral, knows only the means, not the end, and leaves us lost in despair—devoid of hope. Thus, the concept that knowledge is power and its unwise use leads to dehumanization and its consequences—death solutions.

Kass mimics Humphry: Let there be nothing but compassion and aid-in-dying for those poor incompetents whose disability or loss of dignity convinces us that they would choose death if they had only mind enough to do so. Thus, the right to choose one's own death becomes quickly mixed-up with the right to choose someone else's.

True autonomy requires a limit to individual rights in order to protect the milieu (society)—the only place where the concept of the rights has any meaning. In essence, individualism and individual freedom are an illusion except in the social context. We are, by nature, obligate moral and social beings.

Therefore, acting in the best interest of the individual and the best interest of the ordering of society, we ought to discourage and disapprove death solutions while providing care and concern in prevention of suicide, compatible with a reasonable limit to the individual's autonomy and develop effective human alternatives.

When it is determined that medical treatment can be

appropriately and ethically withheld or withdrawn, the decision to allow-to-die must not be involuntary but must be motivated as an act of respect for life, provide meaningful symbolism and due regard and consideration of spiritual purpose; not as aid-in-dying to speed the process of death.

Our choice as physicians is: We can assert the patient's life is devoid of value, lacks intrinsic worth and dignity, is no longer truly human, and provide aid-in-dying, *or* we can help vulnerable individuals in despair by re-asserting that their life, because they are human, has intrinsic worth and dignity and provide them compassionate, palliative care, and hope.

Conclusion

My conclusion is that physicians and the medical profession should provide aid-in-living not aid-in-dying. Providing moral, social, cultural, and legal justification for a right to suicide, the suicidal act and condoned and/or assisted suicide, i.e., active voluntary euthanasia, can only lead to increased individual and social pathology—involuntary euthanasia, both passive and active. To cease efforts to prevent suicide and to encourage the suicide of the terminally ill, the disabled, the chronically ill, the handicapped, and the elderly constitutes social Darwinism. Our success in preventing suicide will reflect how, as a culture, we turn from efforts to improve our lives together toward the lesser good of helping each other die.

Summary

There are reasonable limits to individual autonomy in ethical decision-making. Personal, moral, social, and cultural constraints, as well as legal sanctions, are justified in addressing the psycho-social and bio-ethical issues of unassisted and assisted suicide—active voluntary euthanasia. The credibility of the pluralistic proposition, the principle of individual autonomy in ethical decision-making, as to crucial human life issues, and the public interest and the common good, requires a robust reconsideration of the personal morality inherent in the notion of an individual autonomous right to suicide. Ethically, I would draw the line *here*.

Organizations

Organizations Involved in Life, Death, and Family Issues

American Family Association, P.O. Drawer 2440, Tupelo, Mississippi 38803. (Media watchdog.)

Americans for a Sound AIDS/HIV Policy, P.O. Box 17433, Washington, D.C. 20041.

American Rights Coalition, P.O. Box 487, Chattanooga, Tennessee 37401. (Abortion injury, legal action.)

Americans United for Life, 343 S. Dearborn Street, Suite 1804, Chicago, Illinois 60604. (Pro-life Law.)

Bethany Christian Services, 901 Eastern Ave., NE, Grand Rapids, Michigan 49503. (Adoption agency.)

Black Americans for Life, 419 7th Street NW, Suite 402, Washington, D.C. 20004.

Center for Applied Christian Ethics, Wheaton College, Wheaton, Illinois 60187. (Biblical ethics.)

Concerned Women for America, 370 L'Enfant Promenade, SW, Suite 800, Washington, D.C. 20035. (Family issues.)

Eagle Forum, P.O. Box 618, Alton, Illinois 62002. (Family and political issues.)

Eternal Perspective Ministries, 2229 East Burnside #23, Gresham, Oregon 97030. (Pro-life issues.)

Exodus International, P.O. Box 2121, San Rafael, California 94912. (Ministry to homosexuals.)

Family Research Council, 700 13th Street NW, Suite 500, Washington, D.C. 20005. (Family issues.)

Family Life Ministries, P.O. Box 2700, Washington, D.C. 20013-2700. (Family issues.)

Focus on the Family, P.O. Box 35500, Colorado Springs, Colorado 80935-3550. (Family issues.)

Human Life International, 7845-E Airpark Blvd., Gaithersburg, Maryland, 20879. (Pro-life and euthanasia issues.)

International Anti-Euthanasia Task Force, The Human Life Center, University of Steubenville, Steubenville, Ohio 43952. (Euthanasia.)

Joni and Friends, P.O. Box 3333, Agoura, California 91301. (Disability advocacy group.)

Legal Rights for Women, P.O. Box 11061, Pensacola, Florida 32524-1061. (Abor

Recommended Reading

Recommended Reading on Life and Death, Feminism and the Family

Alcorn, Randy. *Pro Life Answers to Pro Choice Arguments*, Portland, OR: Multnomah Press, 1993.

Ankerberg, John and John Weldon. *When Does Life Begin?* Nashville, TN: Wolgemuth & Hyatt Publishers, 1989.

Bauer, Gary. *Free to be Family*, Washington, D.C.: Family Research Council, 1992.

Biebel, David, Robert Orr, David L. Schiedermayer. *Life and Death Decisions*, Colorado Springs, CO: Nav Press, 1990.

Bell, Ruth. *Changing Bodies, Changing Lives*, New York, NY: Vintage Books, 1988.

Binding, Dr. Karl and Prof. Dr. Alfred Hoche. *Permitting the Destruction of Unworthy Life*, National Center for the Medically Dependent and Disabled, Inc., reprint, 1993.

Blocher, Mark. *Vital Signs–Decisions That Determine The Quality of Life and Health*, Chicago, IL: Moody Press, 1992.

Cameron, Nigel de S. *The New Medicine: Life and Death After Hippocrates*, Wheaton, IL: Crossway Books, 1992.

Caplan, Arthur. *Compelled Compassion: Government Intervention in the Treatment of Critically Ill Newborns*, Totowa, NJ: Humana Press, 1992.

Caplan, Arthur. *When Medicine Went Mad: Bioethics and the Holocaust*, Totowa, NJ: Humana Press, 1992.

Carlson, Allan C. *Family Questions: Reflections on the American Social Crisis*, New Brunswick, NJ: Transaction Books, 1988.

Colson, Charles. *Against the Night: Living in the New Dark Ages*, Ann Arbor, MI: Vine Books, 1989.

Colson, Charles. *Kingdoms in Conflict*, Zondervan Publishing Co., Grand Rapids, MI: Zondervan Publishing Co., 1987.

Recommended Reading

Cundiff, David. *Euthanasia is NOT the Answer*, Totowa, NJ: Humana Press, 1992.

Dobson, James and Gary Bauer. *Children at Risk*, Dallas, TX: Word Publishing, 1990.

Donohue, William. *The New Freedom: Individualism and Collectivism in the Social Lives of Americans*, New Brunswick, NJ: Transaction Books, 1990.

Everett, Carol. *Blood Money*, Portland, OR: Multnomah Press, 1992.

Geisler, Norman. *Christian Ethics: Options and Issues*, Grand Rapids, MI: Baker Book House, 1989.

Geisler, Norman. *Matters of Life and Death*, Grand Rapids, MI: Baker Book House, 1991.

Gilder, George. *Sexual Suicide*, New York, NY: Bantam Books, 1975.

Grant, George. *Grand Illusions: The Legacy of Planned Parenthood*, Brentwood, TN: Wolgemuth & Hyatt, 1988.

Horan, Dennis J. *Infanticide and the Handicapped Newborn*, Provo, UT: Brigham Young University Press, 1982.

Humphry, Derek. *Final Exit*, Eugene, OR: The Hemlock Society, 1991.

Kassian, Mary A. *The Feminist Gospel*, Wheaton, IL: Crossway Books, 1992.

Kass, Leon R. *Toward a More Natural Science: Biology and Human Affairs*, New York, NY: Free Press, 1985.

Kevorkian, Jack. *Prescription: Medicide, The Goodness of Planned Death*, Buffalo, NY: Prometheus Books, 1991.

Kreeft, Peter. *Making Choices: Finding Black and White in a World of Grays*, Ann Arbor, MI: Servant Publications, 1990.

Kurtz, Paul. *Humanist Manifestos I and II*, Buffalo, NY: Prometheus Books, 1973.

Levin, Michael. *Feminism and Freedom*, New Brunswick, NJ: Transaction Books, 1987.

Lifton, Robert Jay. *The Nazi Doctors: Medical Killing and the Psychology of Genocide*, New York, NY: Basic Books, 1986.

Marker, Rita. *Deadly Compassion*, New York, NY: William Morrow and Company, 1993.

McGraw, Onalee. *The Family, Feminism and the Therapeutic State*, Washington, D.C.: The Heritage Foundation, 1980.

McIlhaney, Joe S. *Safe Sex*, Grand Rapids, MI: Baker Book House, 1992.

Mosbacker, Barrett L. *School Based Clinics and Other Critical Issues in Public Education*, Westchester, IL: Crossway Books, 1987.

Nathanson, Bernard. *Aborting America*, Garden City, NY: Doubleday & Co., 1979.

Noebel, David A. *Understanding the Times: The Story of the Biblical Christian, Marxist/Leninist and Secular Humanist Worldviews*, Manitou Springs, CO: Summit Press, 1991.

Olasky, Marvin. *Abortion Rites*, Wheaton, IL: Crossway Books, 1992.

Olasky, Marvin and Susan Olasky. *More Than Kindness: A Compassionate Approach to Crisis Childbearing*, Westchester, IL: Crossway Books, 1990.

Ramsey, Paul. *The Ethics of Fetal Research*, New Haven, CT: Yale University Press, 1975.

Reagan, Ronald. *Abortion and the Conscience of the Nation*, Nashville, TN: Thomas Nelson Publishers, 1984.

Rausch, David. *A Legacy of Hatred: Why Christians Must Not Forget the Holocaust*,

Grand Rapids, MI: Baker Book House, 1990.

Schaeffer, Francis. *Whatever Happened to the Human Race?*, Old Tappan, NJ: Fleming H. Revell Company, 1979.

Schemmer, Kenneth E. *Tinkering with People*, Wheaton, IL: Victor Books, 1992.

Skoglund, Elizabeth. *Life on the Line*, Wheaton, IL: Tyndale House, 1992.

Spring, Beth, and Ed Larson. *Euthanasia*, Portland, OR: Multnomah Press, 1988.

Sproul, R.C. *Abortion: A Rational Look at an Emotional Issue*, Colorado Springs, CO: Nav Press, 1990.

Tada, Joni Eareckson. *When Is It Right to Die?*, Grand Rapids, MI: Zondervan Publishing, 1992.

Thomas, Cal. *The Death of Ethics in America*, Dallas, TX: Word Publishing, 1988.

Whitehead, John. *The Second American Revolution*, Wheaton, IL: Crossway Books, 1982.

Whitehead, John. *Parents Rights*, Wheaton, IL: Crossway Books, 1985.

Whitehead, John. *The Stealing of America*, Wheaton, IL: Crossway Books, 1983.

Notes

Chapter One

1. Dr. Karl Binding and Professor Dr. Alfred Hoche, *Releasing Persons from Lives Devoid of Value*, as quoted in Robert Jay Lifton, *The Nazi Doctors* (New York: Basic Books, 1986), 47.

2. James Watson, as quoted in C. Everett Koop, "Ethical and Surgical Considerations" in *Infanticide* (Provo, UT: Brigham Young University Press, 1982), 97.

3. Nigel de S. Cameron, *The New Medicine: Life and Death After Hippocrates* (Wheaton, IL: Crossway Books, 1992), 162.

4. Ibid., 60.

5. John Whitehead, *The Stealing of America* (Wheaton, IL: Crossway Books, 1983), 52-53.

6. Ibid.

7. John Whitehead, *The Second American Revolution* (Wheaton, IL: Crossway Books, 1982), 141.

Chapter Two

1. Dr. Karl Binding and Prof. Dr. Alfred Hoche, *Releasing Persons from Lives Devoid of Value*, as quoted in Robert Jay Lifton, *The Nazi Doctors* (New York: Basic Books, 1986), 47.

2. Nigel de S. Cameron, *The New Medicine: Life and Death after Hippocrates* (Wheaton, IL: Crossway Books, 1992).

3. Dr. Leo Alexander, "Medical Science Under Dictatorship," *New England Journal of Medicine* (14 July 1949): 39.

4. Ibid., 40.

5. Lifton, *The Nazi Doctors*, 445.

6. Alexander, "Medical Science," 44.
7. Ibid., 45.
8. John Whitehead, *The Stealing of America* (Wheaton, IL: Crossway Books, 1983), 42.

Chapter Three

1. Dr. Lois Lobb as quoted in Frank York, "Beware Convenience Killing," *The Review of the News* (19 March 1975): 3.
2. Ibid.
3. Dr. Timothy Quill, et al, "Care of the Hopelessly Ill: Proposed Clinical Criteria

Chapter Four

1. Phyllis Schafly, "What Really Happened in Houston," 1977.
2. "Proposed National Plan of Action," National Women's Conference, Houston, TX 18-21 (November 1977).
3. Michael Levin, *Feminism and Freedom* (New Brunswick, NJ: Transaction Books, 1988), 187.
4. Dr. James Dobson, *Children at Risk* (Waco, TX: Word, Inc. 1990), 156.
5. Ibid.
6. Dr. Harold Voth, *Real Men* (Lafayette, LA: Huntington House Publishers, 1993), forthcoming.
7. Dr. Judith Reisman, *Soft Porn Plays Hardball* (Lafayette, LA: Huntington House Publishers, 1991).
8. Gary Bauer, *Free to be Family* (Washington DC: Family Research Council 1992), 25.
9. Ibid., 23.
10. Douglas A. Smith and G. Poger Jarjoura, "Social Structure and Criminal Victimization," *Journal of Research on Crime and Delinquency* 25 (February 1988), 27-52.
11. Bauer, *Free*, 30.
12. Dr. Joe S. McIlhaney, *Sexuality and Sexually Transmitted Diseases* (Grand Rapids, MI: Baker Book House, 1990), 14-15.
13. Bauer, *Free*, 77.
14. Ibid., 78.
15. Ibid.
16. Ibid., 87.
17. Dr. Jerome A. Motto, "Suicide is an Individual Right," *Problems of Death: Opposing Viewpoints*, ed. David L. Bender (Minneapolis, MN: Greenhaven Press, 1981), as quoted in Bauer, *Free*, 88.
18. Henry J. Redd, M.D., "The American Academy of Pediatrics Policy Statement on Contraception and Adolescence: A Dissent," *Concerned Women for America Newsletter* (July 1990), 16.

Chapter Five

1. F.V. Scott, "The New American Gothic Planned Parenthood," *Passport Magazine* (July-August 1988), 7.

2. Ibid., 6.

3. Ibid., 7.

4. Dr. George Grant, *Grand Illusions: The Legacy of Planned Parenthood* 2d ed. (Franklin, TN: Adroit Press, 1992), 96.

5. Scott, "The New American Gothic," 8.

6. Ibid.

Chapter Six

1. James Watson, as quoted in C. Everett Koop, "Ethical and Surgical Considerations" in *Infanticide* (Provo, UT: Brigham Young University Press, 1982), 97.

2. Francis Crick as quoted in Koop, "Ethical Considerations," 97.

3. Joseph Fletcher as quoted in Koop, "Ethical Considerations," 96-97.

4. *Pediatrics* (October 1977).

5. Policy Statement, American Academy of Pediatrics Committee on Bioethics, August 1983.

Chapter Seven

1. "Cancer-stricken man received suicide aid," *Colorado Springs Gazette Telegraph* (21 January 1993): A6.

2. UPI Report, 12 November 1992.

3. Nancy Gibbs, "Mercy's Friend or Foe?" *Time Magazine* (28 December 1992): 37.

4. Rita Marker, "Euthanasia: A Historical Overview," *Maryland Journal of Contemporary Legal Issues* 2 (Summer 1991): 280.

5. Ibid.

6. Ibid.

7. Justice Antonin Scalia writing on *Nancy Cruzan, by her parents and co-guardians Lester L. Cruzan, Petitioners, v. Director, Missouri Department of Health, et al*, on writ of certiorari to the Supreme Court of Missouri, 25 June 1990.

8. David Llewellyn Jr., "Licensed to Kill, Life and Liberty," 2.

9. Robin Bernhoft, "Is It Merciful to Kill?"

10. Dr. David Cundff, *Euthanasia Is Not the Answer* (Totowa, NJ: The Humana Press, Inc., 1992), 7.

11. Ibid., 129.

12. Ibid., 162.

Chapter Eight

1. Dr. Joe S. McIlhaney Jr., *Sexuality and Sexually Transmitted Diseases* (Grand Rapids, MI: Baker Book House, 1990), 34.

2. Statistics compiled from *American Journal of Nursing* (October 1987): 1306; Dr. Charles M. Roland, Naval Research Laboratories, Chemistry Division, Washington, D.C. (September 1992); Centers for Disease Control; Food and Drug Administration.

3. "Hospitals detaining TB patients for treatment," *Colorado Springs Gazette Telegraph* (28 November 1992): A6.

4. Chuck and Donna McIlhenny with Frank York, *When the Wicked Seize a City* (Lafayette, LA: Huntington House Publishers, 1993), 102.

5. *Colorado Springs Gazette Telegraph*, A6.

6. D.E. Woodhouse, et al, "Restricting personal behavior: case studies on legal measures to prevent the spread of HIV," *International Journal of STD and AIDS* (March/April 1993): A251/1-4.

7. Ibid.

Chapter Nine

1. Dr. James Hitchcock, "Competing Ethical Systems," *Catholic League Newsletter* 8 (1981): 1.

2. Nigel de S. Cameron, *The New Medicine: Life and Death after Hippocrates* (Wheaton, IL: Crossway Books, 1992), 163.

3. William Donohoe, *The New Freedom: Individualism and Collectivism in the Social Lives of Americans* (New Brunswick, NJ: Transaction Books, 1990), 8.

Chapter Ten

1. Dr. Karl Binding and Prof. Dr. Alfred Hoche, *Permitting the Destruction of Unworthy Life* (Terre Haute, IN: National Legal Center for the Medically Dependent and Disabled, 1993), reprint.

2. Dr. Leo Alexander, "Medical Science Under Dictatorship," *New England Journal of Medicine* (14 July 1949): 44.

3. Dr. Richard Fenigsen, "Euthanasia in The Netherlands," *Issues in Law and Medicine* (Winter 1990): 229.

4. Ibid., 230.

5. Ibid., 242.

6. Ibid., 240.

7. Ibid., 239.

8. John Keown, "Dutch Slide Down Euthanasia's Slippery Slope," *National Right to Life News* (4 February 1992): 17.

HUNTINGTON HOUSE PUBLISHERS
RECENT RELEASES

Loyal Opposition:
A Christian Response to the Clinton Agenda
by John Edismoe

The night before the November 1992 elections, a well-known evangelist claims to have had a dream. In this dream, he says, God told him that Bill Clinton would be elected President, and Christians should support his Presidency. **What are we to make of this?** Does it follow that, because God **allowed** Clinton to be President; therefore, God **wants** Clinton to be president? Does God **want** everything that God **allows**? Is it possible for an event to occur even though that event displeases God? **How do we stand firm in our opposition to the administration's proposals when those proposals contradict Biblical values?** And how do we organize and work effectively for constructive action to restore our nation to basic values?

ISBN 1-56384-044-8 $7.99

When the Wicked Seize a City
by Chuck & Donna McIlhenny with Frank York

A highly publicized lawsuit . . . a house fire-bombed in the night . . . the shatter of windows smashed by politically motivated vandals cuts into the night. . . . All this because Chuck McIlhenny voiced God's condemnation of a behavior and life-style and protested the destruction of society that results from its practice. That behavior is homosexuality, and that life-style is the gay culture. This book explores: the rise of gay power and what it will mean if Christians do not organize and prepare for the battle.

ISBN 1-56384-024-3 $9.99

A Jewish Conservative Looks at Pagan America
by Don Feder

Don Feder's pen finds its targets in the enemies of God, family, and American tradition and morality. Deftly . . . delightfully . . . the master allegorist and Titian with a typewriter brings clarity to the most complex sociological issues and evokes giggles and wry smiles from both followers and foes. Feder is Jewish to the core, and he finds in his Judaism no inconsistency with an American Judeo-Christian ethic.

ISBN 1-56384-036-7 Trade Paper $9.99
ISBN 1-56384-037-5 Hardcover $19.99

Gays & Guns—The Case Against Homosexuals in the Military
by John Eidsmoe

The homosexual revolution seeks to overthrow the Laws of Nature. A Lieutenant Colonel in the United States Air Force Reserve, Dr. John Eidsmoe eloquently contends that admitting gays into the military would weaken the combat effectiveness of our armed forces. This cataclysmic step would also legitimize homosexuality, a lifestyle that most Americans know is wrong.

While echoing Cicero's assertion that "a sense of what is right is common to all mankind," Eidsmoe rationally defends his belief. There are laws that govern the universe, he reminds us. Laws that compel the earth to rotate on its axis, laws that govern the economy; and so there is also a moral law that governs man's nature. The violation of this moral law is physically, emotionally and spiritually destructive. It is destructive to both the individual and to the community of which he is a member.

ISBN Trade Paper 1-56384-043-X $7.99
ISBN Hardcover 1-56384-046-4 $14.99

Trojan Horse—
How the New Age Movement Infiltrates the Church
by Samantha Smith & Brenda Scott

New Age/Occult techniques are being introduced into all major denominations. The revolution is subtle, cumulative, and deadly. Through what door has this heresy entered the church? The authors attempt to demonstrate that Madeleine L'Engle has been and continues to be a major New Age source of entry into the church.

ISBN 1-56384-040-5 $9.99